SEXUALITY IN INDIA
Teenager and Teacher

SEXUALITY IN INDIA
Teenager and Teacher

Dr. KAVITA JOSHI

KALPAZ PUBLICATIONS
Delhi-110 052

SEXUALITY IN INDIA: Teenager and Teacher

(Education)

ISBN: 81-7835-253-2

Published in 2004 in India by
Kalpaz Publications
C-30, Satyawati Nagar
Delhi-110052
E-mail : kalpaz@hotmail.com

Lasertypesetting by: Varsha Graphics, Delhi
Printed by: Mehra Offset Press, Delhi

Contents

Foreword

Sex and sexuality have been culturally sensitive and considered private matters not to be discussed in public. Which is why in spite of the demands being made through various sources for the introduction of sex education in the school curriculum, a decision to move in that direction continued to be postponed for long. For the first time, the *National Curriculum for Elementary and Secondary Education: A Framework*, prepared by National Council of Education Research and Training (NCERT) in 1988 as a follow up of the National Policy on Education 1986 contained a separate objective on sexual behaviour. But concerted efforts in this area were initiated only in 1993 when in the process of evolving a national consensus in its favour the new curricular area was named as adolescence education. The latest National Curriculum Framework for School Education prepared by NCERT in 2000 also contains the objective stated in the 1988 Framework and provides guidelines for the integration of these concerns in the content and process of school education.

Whereas various kinds of activities are being conduced to facilitate and promote the integration of elements related to sex and sexuality in the school curriculum, one of the major constraints has been lack of authentic data base on the needs of adolescents are identified on the basic on the findings of selected numbers of studies of the perceptions of those needs who plan the interventions.

The present publication, *Sexuality in India: Teenagers and Teacher fills* in a significant gap. It provides empirically tested data in respect of not only the perceptions of sex and sexuality by adolescents and their teachers but also their values towards toward these concerns. Although the book is an outcome of an empirical study conduced on a manageable sample, its findings have larger implications. It may prove to be a very significant addition to the growing literature on adolescents and may be useful for educational planners, curriculum developments, teacher educators and researchers.

J.C Pandey
Project Coordinator
National Population Education Project
National Council of Educational Research and Training, New Delhi

Preface

The present book titled as *Sexuality in India: Teenagers and Teachers* is based on my research study "Values and Perceptions of Adolescent Students and Their Teachers Relating to Sex and Sexuality". Purpose of this book is two fold: first to introduce the reader to the field of adolescence education; and second to present him with meaningful interpretations of this study.

In the opening chapter I have discussed the important phase of life 'Adolescence' and its characteristics. Why there is a need of an area called Adolescence education? What is the meaning of sex and sexuality? How various values and perceptions are linked to sex and sexuality? Need of adolescence education is especially meaningful today when they are in a world full of information about sex and sexuality on TV, internet, media, films and footpath literature. Which one is right or wrong? This judgement has to exercised according to their own set of value and perceptions about sex and sexuality. Varied views, everchanging values disturb and confuse the people who are in critical phase of development. They look up to the society, adults, parents, role model and teachers for any suggestions. If the suggestions coming are contradictory, they add to the confusion. I have drawn upon research studies that have more than usual amount of relevance for students and researchers.

In second chapter I have reviewed literature from India and abroad. It includes abstracts of material developed for adolescence education, articles from published world and research findings of several studies. Third chapter details about the research design and development of the tool on values and perceptions of) sex and sexuality.

Chapter four presents the data, its statistical analysis and results. I have drawn upon research studies that have more than usual amount of relevance for readers. Research findings of other studies have been seen for their relevance, supporting or contradictory findings. I have attempted to do this while giving judicious coverage to the main theme.

Complete index and Bibliography has been given for further reference.

For myself, the writing of this book has been an interesting and stimulating experience. Working and knowing variety of adolescent cultures have given me a special appreciation for research findings of human sexual behaviour. This can aid our understanding of the problems and issues in everyday life. Dealing with adolescents in particular has given me an opportunity to share some of my interests for the field.

I am thankful to my supervisor Prof. R.S. Khan, Dr. J.L.N. Pandey, Dr. N. Hasnain and Dr. B.S. Nagi for all the encouragement and stimulating exchange of ideas. I am particularly indebted to my family for the patience they have shown during writing of this book. Preparing the manuscript was very easy and enjoyable work with Mr. Vikas.

6th September 2003 **Dr. Kavita Joshi**

Acknowledgments

It is with deep reverence, I wish to acknowledge my sincere gratitude to my supervisor Prof. Riaz Shakir Khan, IASE, Jamia Millia Islamia, New Delhi, who with a long experience in the area of Population Education has guided my efforts at all stages of the work presented in this thesis. His clear thinking, sharp understanding and sympathetic nature inspired the investigator at every step to work hard. His openness to new ideas and giving them his experienced support has stimulated me to the study. Inspite of his heavy and manifold duties, he always found time to attend to my problems. Without his sincere devotion, constant encouragement and sustained interest in my work, this study would not have been completed.

I owe a debt of gratitude to Dr. J.L. Pandey, National Coordinator, NPEP, DESSH, NCERT, New Delhi who has provided persistent guidance and encouragement through out my study. I express a deep sense of gratitude to Dr. Hasnain, Department of Psychology, Jamia Millia Islamia for his valuable suggestions during my study.

I express my indebtedness to the Education Officer, Shri Sachikant, Kendriya Vidyalaya Sangathan for his kind permission to do this doctoral level research work which will go a long way in my professional growth.

I express my indebtedness to Dr. B.S. Nagi, Director, CSD, Lodhi Estate, New Delhi for his valuable suggestions for the processing of data and getting the data analysed.

I would also like to thank the Principals and staff of the schools who cooperated with me for data collection from their schools. I also acknowledge my indebtedness to scholars, educationists and psychologists whose books on education, psychology and research have been utilized by me in the present study.

I owe my gratitude to the ICSSR for the financial support provided for this research work.

The culmination of this research endeavour could not have been achieved without the moral support and cooperation of my family members.

My special thanks go to my parents Shri J.R. Sharma and Mrs. Nirmal, my husband Dr. Deepak Joshi, my daughters, Apoorva, and Soumya, Reena and other family members who had to sacrifice a lot due to my over busy schedule during my research work.

I have deep sense of appreciation for Mr. Vikas Arora, whose coordination could lead to a well-typed report of the study.

Kavita Joshi

1

Introduction

1.1 The Problem

Human behaviour is very complex and when it pertains to sex and sexuality, its complexity increases manifold. All of us feel how difficult it is to be reasonable about sex, although, it is regarded as a treasured sublime instinct of human beings. It denotes the physical and mental traits that distinguish between males and females; and also the physiology and psychological processes related to procreation and sensual pleasure (Goldenson, 1984). Given this understanding, sexual behaviour should have been treated by human societies like any other aspect of human behaviour. But because of taboos and inhibitions attached to it, sex has been an emotionally disturbing topic. If we have to discuss it face-to-face, there is an embarrassment and there are prudent silences. We prefer to keep our reflections to ourselves. This has been so because in all human societies sex has been considered a purely private matter and discussion on it publicly has been prescribed by them as improper and unacceptable. Societies have allowed this area of human concern to remain shrouded in mystery.

But sexual development is an integral part of human growth and development and all humans have been inquisitive about it. Since they have not been obtaining information about it openly and directly from legitimate sources and through accurate and authentic channels, and getting it through whatever sources and channels are available, mostly hidden. Clandestine sources have been providing not only inaccurate but also distorted information, generating and reinforcing myths and misconceptions about sex.

The ignorance or false and inaccurate information about sex and sexuality has been adversely affecting not only individuals but also the entire process of social development. It is in this context that the need for sex education particularly for the young people has been seriously felt. There are countries where this education was launched four or five decades ago. In other countries, it was considered important when education in sex related matters became essential with a view to preventing the spread of AIDS pandemic. In countries like India the process of imparting such an education has been initiated very recently. All the critical concerns related to sex and sexuality, reproductive health, HIV/AIDS and drug abuse have been integrated into a broad conceptual framework of adolescence education, and efforts are afoot to make it an integral part of the content and process of the Indian education system.

1.2. Adolescence Education

The term, adolescence education was used for the first time when the UNESCO Principal Regional Office for Asia and the Pacific published a Package on sex and sexuality containing four modules – physical aspect, social aspect, sex roles and sexually transmitted diseases. It named the Package as Adolescence Education (UNESCO, PROAP, 1992). However, this concept was operationalised in India when the National Council of Educational Research and Training (NCERT) organised a National Seminar on Adolescence Education in April 1993. The main objective of the seminar was also to evolve a consensus on the issue of the introduction of sex education in the school curriculum. That is why, it was felt by many that the term 'Adolescence Education' was being used as a euphemism of sex education with a view to enhancing the acceptability of this sensitive education area.

But during the course of the development of the conceptual framework of adolescence education, it became abundantly clear that the concept of adolescence education is broader than that of sex education, as it incorporates all the critical concerns of the period of adolescence. The conceptual framework was developed around three crucial components, viz. Process of growing up from childhood to adulthood, HIV/AIDS and Drug abuse.

This exercise was undertaken on the recommendations of the National Seminar for the introduction of adolescence education in the school curriculum (NCERT, 1994).

Adolescence Sexuality

Perhaps no single event during the adolescent years has as dramatic or widespread effect as the realization of sexuality. The lives of both males and females become wrapped in this new dimension. Adolescence is a time of sexual exploration and experimentation of sexual fantasies and sexual realities, of incorporating sexuality into one's identity. It is not surprising, then, that the adolescent's emerging sexuality causes adjustment problems. Adolescence is the life stage between childhood and adulthood. Its age limits are differently specified, but it extends roughly from age twelve to the late teens, when the physical growth is nearly complete. Puberty is a term often confused with adolescence, occurs at the end of childhood and last from two to four years. It is the period of adolescent during which an individual reaches sexual maturity. Adolescent sexuality examines the physical, psychological and behavioural changes that occurs as the individual leaves childhood, acquires sexual maturity and incorporates the various aspects of sexuality into his or her identity. This emerging sexuality may cause adjustment problems, which may be moderate to severe.

Human beings grow most rapidly at two times during their lives; first, they are six months old and again during adolescent. The second period of accelerated growth is often referred to as the adolescent growth spurt. Adolescents grow both in height and weight, with the increase in height occurring first. As they gain weight, the amount and distribution of fat in their body change, and the proportion of bone and muscle tissue increases. In girls, the adolescent growth spurt usually beings between the ages of nine and eleven and reaches a peak at an average of twelve-and-a-half years. Then growth slows and usually ceases completely between the ages of fifteen of eighteen. The growth spurt in boys generally begins about two years later than it does in girls and lasts for a longer time. It begins between the ages of eleven and fourteen and reaches a peak at about age fifteen, and slowly declines until the age of nineteen or twenty.

The teenager's body grows at differing rates, so that at times adolescents look a bit awkward. Big feet and long legs are the early signs of a changing body, but even these changes do not occur at the same time. First the hands and feet grow, then the arms and legs, later do the shoulders and chest grow to fit the rest of the developing body. Changes in the body proportion become obvious. The trunk widens in the hips and shoulders and the waist line narrows. Boys tend to broaden mostly in the shoulders, girls in the hips.

Puberty is chiefly characterised by sexual development. Sexual development can be best understood by examining the maturation of primary and second sex characteristics. Primary sex characteristics are the physiological features of the sex organs. For males, these organs are thepenis and the testes. For females, they are the ovaries, uterus, clitoris and vagine. Secondary sex characteristics are not directly related to the sexual organs but nevertheless distinguish a mature male from a mature female. Examples of secondary sex characteristics are the male beard and the female breats.

In girls, the onset of breat development is usually, but not always, the first signal that puberty has begun. This typically occurs between the ages of ten and eleven, but can occur as late as ages thirteen and fourteen. There is simultaneous development of uterus and vagina, with enlargement of labia and clitoris. Menarche although perhaps the most dramatic and symbolic sign of girl's changing status, occurs relatively late in puberty, after the growth spurt has reached its peak velocity. The first menstrual periods tends to be irregular, and ovulation does not usually begin until a year or so after menarche.

The first noticeable change in boys is usually growth of the testes and scrotum. The growth of genitals begins, on average, about the age of twelve and is completed, on average, by about the age of fifteen. Boys generally become capable of ejaculation about a year after the penis begins to grow. These first emissions may occur as a result of nocturnal emissions, the ejaculation of semen during sleep. Nocturnal emissions are a normal phase of development and are frequently caused by sexual excitation in dreams or by some type of physical conditions, such as a full bladder.

The adolescents' bodies become more adultlike, their interest in sexual behaviour increases sharply. They must learn the necessary behaviour to satisfy that interest, and they must face the issue of mature gender identify. This includes the expression of sexual needs and feelings and the acceptance or rejection of sex roles. The onset of dating and the beginning of physical intimacies with the opposite sex can provoke frustration and anxiety. As this unfamiliar territory is explored, the adolescent is often very underinformed and overly self-conscious. Conflicting sexual values and messages are frequently encountered, accentuating the problem of integrating sexual drives with other aspects of personality.

Adolescents are actually aware of the rapid changes taking places in their bodies. How they react to such changes greatly affect how they evaluate themselves. It is in this manner that physical and psychological developments are related. Physical changes may cause psychological discomfort. Adolescents are particularly concerned about whether they are of the "right" shape or size and whether they measure upto the "ideal" adolescent. Rapid growth, awkwardness, acne, voice changes, menarche, and other developments which produce emotional distress. Therefore, it is not surprising that the timing of physical and sexual maturity may have an important influence on psychological adjustment. Adolescents are generally concerned about anything that sets them apart from their peers. Being either the first or the last to go through puberty can cause considerable self-consciousness.

In general, boys who mature early have a distinct advantage over those who mature late. They tend to be more poise, easy-going and good nature. They, are taller, heavier and more muscular than other boys of their age. They are also more likely to excel at sports, achieve greater popularity and become school leaders. In contract, late-maturing boys not only are smaller and less well-developed in their age groups, but they also are not as interest in dating. When they become interested in girls, they often lack social skills, and are likely to feel inadequate, anxious and self-conscious. These personality characteristics tend to persist into early childhood, although they become less marked and often disappear with the time.

For girls, early maturation appears to be a mixed blessing. Girls who mature early grow taller, develop breats, and go through menarche as much six years before some of their peers. Their larger size and more adult physique may make them feel conspicuous and awkward, while at the same time they may be popular with the boys and experience more dating opportunity. They also may have to deal with parents and guardians who have reacted to their early sexual development by being overly restrictive. For these reasons, the late-maturing girls often finds adolescence a little easier than her early-maturing peer. As with boys, the consequences of early and late maturation decrease over time.

Sexual maturation has other psychological consequences as well. In particular, patterns of sexual behaviour change tremendously with the arrival of sexual maturity. As adolescents' bodies become more adult, their interest in sexual behaviour increases sharpl, as they explore their identities, they develop a sexual script, or a stereotyped pattern for how individuals should behave sexually.

The sexual scripts for boys is frequently different than the sexual script for girls. As a result, male and female generally think differently about sex. This discrepancy can cause problems and confusion for adolescents as they struggle with their sexual identities. For males, the focus of sexuality may be sexual conquest, to the point that young men who are nonexploitative or inexperienced may be labeled with negative terms. Males are more likely than females to see intercourse as a way of establishing their maturity and of achieving social status. As a consequence, boys are more likely to have sex with someone who is a relative stranger, to have more sexual partners and to disassociate sex from love and emotional intimacy.

Adolescent girls are much more likely than adolescent males to link sexual intercourse with love. The quality of relationships between girls and her partner is a important factor. Most females would agree than sexual intercourse is acceptable if two people are in love and is not acceptable if the two people are not in a romantic relationship. Consequently, females are less likely than males to list pleasures, pleasing their partner, and relieving sexual tension as reasons for having sex.

Given their different sexual motives, boys generally expect sex sooner in a relationship than girl. Since girls usually want to wait until an emotional commitment and intimacy have development. They feel pressured into having sex before they are ready. Therefore, girls may be somewhat uncomfortable with a decision to engage in sexual intercourse.

During the past several decades, attitudes toward sexual activity have changed dramatically. Views regarding premarital sex, extramarital sex and specific sexual acts are probably more open and permissive today than they have been at any time in recent history. Young people are exposed to sexual stimuli on TV and in magazines and motion pictures to a greater extent than ever before. Effective methods of birth control have lessened the fear of pregnancy. All these changes have given the adolescents more freedom. These changes also produce more conflict, however, since guidelines for "appropriate behaviour" are less clear cut than they were in the past. In some families, diversions between adolescent and parental standards of sexual morality is great.

Sexual behaviour as a subject for scientific investigation has traditionally met with much resistance. Historically, the majority of individuals in the fields of medicine and psychology have not considered sex to be appropriate topic for investigation. As a result, knowledge regarding this important dimension of life has been slow to develop. Only since the 1940's have researchers been able to explore the physical psychological aspects of the human sexuality objectively.

Sigmund Freud, the father of psychodynamic theory was one of the first scientists to demonstrate the influence of sexuality in human life. He clearly described the existence of sexuality in infants and children and developed a detailed theory of psychosexual development. Although his theory has been criticized, his rich observations and concepts have had a great impact on psychological thinking. At about the same time that Freud was developing his ideas, Havelock Ellis was publishing a seven volume series called Studies on the Psychology of Sex (1897-1928). Ellis, an English Physician, devoted much of his life to sexual research. He focussed varied nature of human sexual behaviour and challenged ideas commonly held at the time. For example, he did not agree that women were basically asexual, and he recognised the common occurrence of masturbation in both sexes.

Alfred Kinsey was another sexologist who has been instrumental in furthering understanding of human sexual behavour. Although severely criticised for his work, Kinsey paved the way for detailed, objective research. He and his colleagues conducted extensive face-to-face interviews with 12,000 people from all segments of the population. This research produced a large amount of detailed data, resulting in the publications of two major works: Sexual behaviour in the Human Male (1948) and Sexual Behaviour in the Human Female (1953).

The research of Kinsey and others focused on interviews and case histories. The goal was to discover how people behaved sexually, addressing such issues as how often and when they engaged in sexual activity as well as specific behaviours involved. Under laboratory conditions, they observed and recorded the details of human sexual activity. In 1966, their findings were published in a report titled *Human Sexual Response.*

Research specifically directed towards the exploration of adolescent sexuality was not seriously undertaken until the 1950's and 1960's. Even the, the few studies that were conducted handled the topic delicately and focused on attitudes rather than behaviour. When behavour was emphasized, age at first intercourse was generally selected as the major variable. Later studies have been more detailed and expansive, however, a paucity of research in this area still exists.

1.2.1 Need for Adolescence Education

Although human beings always needed accurate knowledge about sex and sexuality, which they have been denied, to manage their sexual behaviour. The human societies have been prescribing norms and there have been values to influence this behaviour, but sex and sexuality being intimately private matter, norms and values have not been observed in their true spirit. The human society has been experiencing incidence of pre-marital and extra-marital sexual relations, pre-marital pregnancies and sexual transmitted diseases. But it has been doggedly ignoring the need to make the authentic information available to individuals through reliable sources.

The ignorance about sex and sexuality, however, did not result in as serious problems as it may do today, primarily because the gap between the onset of puberty and the age at marriage was generally very small. Individuals used to enter into adulthood directly from childhood. The agricultural economy demanded the contribution from many hands to have agricultural production and boys and girls during their childhood itself started helping their parents in agricultural as well as domestic works. The children were generally driven into adult roles, particularly when they got married quite early in their lives.

But situation today is very different. Because of a number of developments, such as the availability of educational opportunities to a large part of the populace, employment outside homes and villages, in industries, open market and government organisations and changing perception of quality of life, have led to the increase in the age of marriage. On the other hand, the age of puberty has been advancing due to better health and nutritional case of children. This has resulted in the fast increasing gap between the age of puberty and the age of marriage. the period between childhood and adulthood, therefore, is now clearly identified as adolescence.

Adolescence is a distinct phase in the age-continuum of human beings, and it coincides with the process of growing up from childhood to adulthood. When children are at the threshold of adolescence, certain hormonal change take place, which are followed by sudden and rapid physical, physiological, psychological and social developments lead to sexual and reproductive maturity in individuals. Generally, the period of adolescence is defined in terms of number of years. Some consider it a period between 13 and 18 years of age, while others put it between 10 and 19 years of age. But adolescence may not be seen in association with the precise number of years, as its periodicity varies from person to person. It is a period of sexual development, during which secondary sexual characteristics appear, grow and develop. It is a period of physical, psychological, intellectual and social maturation from childhood and adulthood, the period extending from puberty to reproductive maturation. (NCERT, 1999)

Adolescents during this period confront a lot of problems. They experience a lot many changes, but are not able to understand those for want of accurate knowledge when they fail to get these information through authentic sources such as family or schools and other educational institutions, they fall back upon the peer group which as ignorant as they are or the cheap literature that spread and reinforce false knowledge, exposing them to myths and misconceptions. Hence, the emphasis is being laid on integration of Adolescence Education inputs into the school curriculum.

1.2.2 Objectives of Adolescence Education

Adolescence Education encompasses human sexuality in its biological, psychological, social, cultural and moral dimensions (NCERT, 1994). UNESCO (1994) has mentioned the following objectives of Adolescence Education:

(i) To provide authentic information and understanding regarding the process of growing upto students according to their age, so as to enable them to cope up with adolescence related problems.

(ii) To promote among students a responsible behaviour towards the opposite sex.

(iii) To inculcate in them an understanding that a happy married life rests on mutual love and affection and on the mutual sharing and caring.

(iv) To help them understand the implications of AIDS pandemic and to make them aware of the causes and ways and means of prevention of HIV infections and other sexually transmitted diseases.

(v) To help them understand the responsibilities of parenthood.

In view of the problems that adolescents have been confronting, there has been growing demand to impart sex education right from the school stage. But this has not been possible so far because of the apprehensions and inhibitions of parents, teachers and educational planners.

It is often argued that by imparting education in respect of sex and sexuality young children will be encouraged to experiment with the newly acquired exciting knowledge. This will lead to promiscuity among them and spoil the social and school environment. Like many other countries, In India also it is argued that it is not appropriate to disturb the innocence of childhood by dealing with sex-related matters (Rubin and Calderwood, 1973).

However, the above mentioned arguments have been adequately considered and found lacking in validity, when the issue of the introduction of adolescence education was subjected to an animated debate nation-wide. It is now increasingly being felt that ignorance in respect of sex-related matters coupled with the inaccurate and false knowledge has been adversely affecting the individual development and generating a number of social problems.

The very foundation of any society rests upon healthy sexual attitudes grounded in appropriate, adequate and accurate sexual information. The orientation towards sex and sexuality are appropriately developed only when individuals have adequate knowledge received through authentic and legitimate channels. Adolescence education is expected to provide such required knowledge to individuals.

It is often stated that the members of the society have so far managed their sexual behaviour, even though they did not receive any education in sex and sexuality. But it is universally realised that the world has been changing, and changing very fast. The social environment is being substantially influenced by the changes and developments in the areas of science and technology, economy, polity, society, culture and way of living during modern times. And hence, the ignorance about sex and sexuality today is claiming greater toll on individuals and society.

Today, in almost all societies the gap between the onset of puberty which is a symbol of sexual maturity and the age at marriage is increasing. The larger is the gap, greater is the possibility of pre-marital sexual relations and related problems. These is now greater need to provide accurate knowledge about sex and sexuality to growing children in their formative years so that they are made aware of the crucial concerns of sexual development and inculcate in them healthy attitudes and desirable value-orientation towards sex and sexuality.

In the absence of adequate knowledge about sex and sexuality, individual behaviour has always been creating problems. but whenever undesirable incidence took place, social institutions like family and community would meticulously put such experiences under the carpet. It was never considered important to take note of the arduous sufferings perpetrated on concerned individuals. Since with the growing potential of the means of communication such incidences are being known and their gravity is realised with great concern. In this context, it is considered essential to empower individuals by making them adequately aware of the implications of sexual behaviour.

It is also observed that the impact of traditional value system that used to influence the sex related behaviour of individuals substantially has been waving because certain new trends in social development such as, urbanisation, migration, social and economic mobility, changing life styles and exposure to the fast expanding media. In this context also there is an urgent need to make educational intervention to revitalise the process of value orientation.

The arrival of AIDS pandemic has created still more urgent need to impart adolescence education to all members of the society and particularly to the young people. since the most potential route of HIV transmission is the sex-related behaviour and since there is neither any preventive vaccine or cure to this pandemic, education is the only preventive measure that can be effective in arresting the spread of AIDS.

The education in these issues was also considered necessary when the International

Conference on Population and Development (ICPD), held in Cairo in 1994 was discussing the critical concerns of reproductive health, particularly the reproductive health needs of adolescents. The Programme of Action adopted by the Conference recommends that adolescents should be adequately informed about reproductive health, so that they attain a level of maturity required to make responsible and informed decisions. (POA, ICPD, 1994)

1.3 Perceptions, Values and Education

The education in sex-related matters is considered essential for more significant reasons than simply providing the knowledge of various aspects of sexual development to the people, and particularly young people. Human behaviour is influenced not only by the knowledge but also, and perhaps more importantly by perceptions and values.

1.3.1 Perception

Perception denotes sensory experience which has gained meaning or significance. When as the result of learning experiences, one understands the relationships of object which were previously raw, undifferentiated sensory experiences, he or she is said to perceive these objects. The non-sensory learning experience which is essential to transforming meaningless sensory experiences into perceptions involves the development of concepts or ideas about the sensory experiences. Perception thus is the awareness of objects, relationships and events via the senses, including such activities as recognising, observing and discriminating. these activities enable us to organise and interpret stimuli we receive into meaningful knowledge of the world. The perception also is greatly influenced by values.

1.3.2 Values

Value, a term frequently referred to in the social sciences, has scores of meanings. Some regard it as "any object, situation, ideal, principle or norms that a person or a group of people consider desirable and worthy." (Zadrozuy, 1959). Goldenson defines value in the Longman Dictionary of Psychology and Psychiatry as "a goal or standard that is considered especially worthy by an individual or society" (Goldenson, 1984)

The concept of value has been explained in yet another way. In most instances of social sciences the word is used only in those cases where an actual interactive relationship exists between needs, attitudes and desires on the one hand and objects on the other. These objects perceived by a scientific observer to have relevance for the needs, attitudes and desires of the people whom he is observing, are not values unless this relevance has somehow been translated into an observable relationship between the thoughts and actions of the people observed and the objects observed (Gould & Kolb, 1964)

However, there is another usage which is perhaps the one most frequently found in sociology and anthropology. The term denotes "the shared cultural standards according to which the relevance – moral, aesthetic, or cognitive-of the objects of attitudes desires, and needs can be compared and judged. There is the belief among those who share a set of such standards that they are valid and should be employed in valuing an object, e.g. relating to needs, desires or attitudes and in evaluating an object, i.e. company its relevance with that of another object or other objects."

Value is what is desired, liked or preferred. It may be a physical object, a quality of mind, a mental state or anything on which liking and preference can be expressed. Values refer to those things that men desire, like or prefer. These values can have wide range from concrete to absolute and abstract ideals influencing the issues relating to marriage, job, house, promotion, friends, responsibilities to social justice, peace, secularism, equality, etc.

Human beings are different from animals, as they are rational. Life gets a meaning and purpose only because they keep on exercising judgement on their motives, desires and actions. This characteristically human quality of critical self-examination leads us to second sense of value, value as objective or as that which promotes a goal independently of one's liking or preferences. Value is objective in the sense that what is of value to one is not necessarily what one likes or wants. In other words, what is desired is not always desirable and what is not desired is actually desirable. Desirable and undesirable are to be judged from the point of view of the goal or end to which an object or action leads. The value that has worth in itself without reference to any end is a higher value called intrinsic value, while instrumental values are means to reach or achieve a higher end or value. There are several other such things (like money) which people value as means to achieve higher things like knowledge, truth, happiness, spiritual perfection, etc. Values can also be classified as those dealing without notions of right or wrong and good or evil and those that refer to our standard of judgement of the beautiful and ugly (aesthetic values). Values can also be referred as positive and negative values and higher and lower values depending on whether they cater to the material or bodily desire or to the higher faculties of man – the intellectual, aesthetic, moral and spiritual. Satisfaction that one gets from pursuit of higher values is intrinsic whereas the lower values lead to instrumental and ephemeral pleasures as the hierarchy of needs is explained by Maslow.

In such a world, there are no absolute or eternal values. All values are relative to particular situations and times. What is good today may not be good tomorrow. What is of a great value here may not be of any value elsewhere. A good act, an ethical act, is measured by the results it yields. A human act produces wider and wider effects as the product of this act flows in to the community. The ultimate test of 'good' is therefore its public consequences. (Sheshadri, 1994)

Another view about values is that human beings are the constructors of values just as they are the constructors of their truths. They test their value claims in experience and so accept them as temporary and tentative. Since values are to be found in the context of experience, individuals will have to find out what they ought to want in the same relativistic circumstances of ordinary experiencing. Individual's valuing is a constant creation of and accommodation to the changing moral environment about him or her. Such a public sharing of values is best fostered in the free and permissive atmosphere of democracy.

Inspite of the bewildering variety of explanations of the concept of value, there has been a broad agreement about its definition. Values are normative standards or criteria which guide human behaviour and decision-making. They serve as guidelines which determine how individuals act upon available choices. They do not exist by themselves but in the minds of human beings and are reflected in the specific judgements or claims people made and in the worth they place on the different aspects of life. When a person claims that certain idea, object, act, interest or behaviour is right and out to be carried out or supported, he or she actually reveals his or her standard or criterion for value judgement. Values develop from the experiences we have, from the influence of people and conditions around us. These values influence our actions, and the consequences of these actions in turn influence our values. All acts of individuals are determined by their respective sets of value. Whenever, thinking takes place, decisions are made, choices are ordered, or preferences expressed, values come into place.

Values originate in the socio-cultural milieu of a given social system and are thus governed by the standards that each social system sets for itself. It is due to this reason that values of one social group differ from those of another. Differing values represent key aspects of variation in human culture. What individuals value is strongly influenced by the specific culture in which they happen to live. These values are internalised by group/society/members in the process of learning called socialisation (Indra, 1992). Socialisation includes all the processes by which anyone from infancy to old age acquires his or her social skills, roles, norms, values and personality patterns which are felt to be vital for their survival and growth. Different cultures have different value systems and these value systems are conditioned by the developments taking place in a cultural setup prove that values have a strong social and cultural base. Society is an ever-evolving system influenced by different agencies of social change.

The set of values in such a society is bound to be influenced with these changes. (Durkheim, 1956)

Values are acquired through the process of socialisation while society itself is ever-changing and ever evolving more so in Indian society which is receptive, flexible and exposed to the changes in world through mass media. Adolescents are more influenced by an adult human model. They learn to develop positive values towards certain people and objects and negative values towards other people and things. These attitudes are susceptible to modification during adulthood, but the process of acquisition and development of value continues. Thus values are formed and learned in relation to identifiable objects both social and non-social. (Sherif & Sherif, 1969)

Children reared in homes where there is strong authoritarianism, ethnic bias and religious bias will very likely carry this to school with them. They may have experiences at school or elsewhere that will produce uncertainty about their prejudices, although many of these persist throughout adulthood. It is the time when child is confronted with children, friends, teachers with different attitudes and beliefs that he or she is likely to encounter cognitive dissonance or blend. These new values blend with his previous set and are reformulated in peer group, school effect of various sources of information also can not be denied.

1.3.3 Sex Related Values

Values have been influencing sexual behaviour of human beings since very early stage of human development, though many a time those have not been obvious (Whiteley, 1967). There have been different sex related values in different societies, and even among different groups in the same society. The interplay of different values is responsible for different sexual behaviour of the individuals of the same group. There are different sets of values in human societies because values are acquired through the process of socialisation while societies themselves have been changing and ever evolving. We find large variations in India itself, e.g. marital relationship between close relations are not permitted in certain communities, it is preferred in others.

About 1500 years ago, in Indian history, 'Kamasutra: The Analytical Treatise on Sex and Love' written by great sage Vatsayana noted that sex socialisation of the youth was undertaken in that period. Until about two hundred years ago, there was little or no separation in the lives of adults and children (Aries, 1962). Since that time, however, the lives of adults have been largely inaccessible to children (Bernstein, 1978). Adolescents in particular have come to develop a life style that is comparatively seeking independence from adults. This independence of adolescents and secretive behaviour of adults has resulted in misunderstanding, conflict and rebellion. This issue of conflict between adolescents and adults is due to difference between desirable and desired behaviour. Different set of values elicits different behaviour from two groups which is more commonly known as 'Generation Gap'.

Sociologists and psychologists maintain that conflict is to be expected and is unavoidable, while other researches feel that the notion of such conflict is a creation of mass media which has responded to the public taste for excitement by exploiting the actions of a majority of adolescents who are disturbed. (Weiner, 1977)

Few of the studies explore the cultural meanings and power relations which guide sexual behaviour of youth. Among the exceptions are two multicentric studies of Family Planning Association of India on Sex Education Counselling Research and Therapy, in 1990 and 1993. (Watsa 1994)

Teachers and parents on their own are by and large, not able to play their role of socialising their children specially in sexual matters properly. (Ruhela, 1969, Inderjeet and Sabina, 1995, Jain, 1995) Hence sexual behaviour is a complex one and may be resultant of one or the other expected value behind it. (Pandey, 2000)

The middle class societies are themselves caught up in the great conflict between tradition and modernity and it is generally toeing the lines dictated by the former. Some of the reasons are illiteracy and poor sex socialisation of parents, timid attitude of teachers and parents on sex related discussions and joint families, etc. (Ruhela, 1969). The Times of India survey also shows that present youth is critical savvy of the changes going in society and media on the name of modernity. (TOI, 1998)

Diverse cultures, languages, customs, beliefs, religions, diets and rapidly changing sexual mores influence their sexual behaviour. Some tribes in India can be quoted for their sex socialisation practices and there are few studies on urban educated youth (FPAI, 1992) but virtually none on rural youth. The few authentic studies on sexual behaviour over the last ten years are generally in relation to family planning and birth control or some surveys by national magaziners but none of the systematic studies are reported on the sex related values in the above said conditions.

Sex related values cover the entire spectrum of sex and sexuality. There are values related to pre-marital sex, abstinence, sex within marriage, outside marriage, homosexuality and so on. But we have been lamenting that the impact of values on human sexual behaviour has been waving.

It is repeatedly observed that the young generation of today is being swayed away by the media and there has been alarming value erosion. They are driving our society towards a permissive society. How much truth lies in such observations is a matter of wild guess, though some studies conducted sporadically have found the increasing incidence of promiscuity among young people. However, it is accepted by one and all that there is no broad database on the basis of which some valid conclusions may be derived.

1.4 Need for the Study

Major changes in society and educational structure go hand in hand. Just as societies evolve, each along entirely different lines and at breathtaking speed, educational change is also necessary not only in the content of what is taught but also in the end result. It gives rise to anxiety among pupils coupled with impatience and, in many cases, open or tacit rejection, because what is presented to them as the 'content of school curricula' fails to provide them with answers to pressing questions which arise from their generations' out look on life but often lie outside their teacher's direct experience. This is more true when matters relate to sex and sexuality. School curricula are a direct reflection of the kind of society in which they are to be found and whose values they represent. It is also true that they provide continuity in the sense that they are drawn up by teacher at the height of its responsibilities and decision making powers, seeks to transmit its specific characteristics to future generations. In situations of rapid and bewildering change the overall reference system of values is often outdated in relation to genuinely innovative situations and changes which mark a break with the past. There are some researches and opinions which suggest that adolescents students show a range of value patterns from traditional views on some issues, confused about other ideas and are yet open to new ideas. They are confused for some issues (relating to premarital sex and girl friend, etc.) at the same time there are some articles that call them as critical savvy and single minded generation. Similarly, teachers see their traditional role of value imparter but are at the same affected equally by the changes taking place in the society in recent years.

Need for sex education has been emphasized rightly by Watsa (1994) as in India sexuality continues to be tied closely to the institution of marriage and to the function of reproduction. Sex is intuitively learnt rather explicitly taught. Sex is learnt through films, media, pornographic material, peer group. The information is often inaccurate and therefore could lead to a series of unwanted outcomes. (Watsa, 1994)

Jeanne Brooks-gunn and Frank Furstenberg (1900), in the book Adolescent Behaviour and Society suggest that numerous issues have received little or no exploration. Included in their list of "research omissions" are the following: frequency of behavours other than intercourse, pubertal education aimed at boys on topics such as ejaculation and condom use, the relation of sexual behaviour to other adolescent behaviour, the meaning of eroticism in adolescents' sex lives, and differences between younger and older adolescents. Social concerns such as teenage pregnancy, sexually transmitted diseases and sex education have focused attention on the need to understand clearly the dynamics of adolescent sexuality. This awareness should encourage broader perspectives for the study of teenage sexual behaviour and produce detailed knowledge sexuality as it occurs in the adolescent experience.

Educational decision makers are increasingly required to deal with the impact of new phenomenon brought about by the combined progress of technology and productivity which affects the human resource aspect (training) and environmental aspect (awareness). Can educational initiatives help to solve the problems related to the sex and sexuality sparked by various values governing their sex behaviour which can be risky in the age of menace of AIDS. Hence, there are special type of education received by school authorities in recent years with emphasis on the word 'education'. Population education, sex education and adolescence education and HIV/AIDS education, are such endeavours.

One of the thrust areas in the Population Education Programme evolved in 1969 was development of right concepts and values relating to sex and sexuality which affected population control (Rao, 1969). Sex education could not get the required acceptance by the society at large and concept was re-evolved in 1992 as Adolescence Education. Objectives of Adolescence Education embraced the objectives of sexuality education. Its importance had been emphasized in NPE, 1986 and also proposed in National Youth Policy 2000. Gopalan (1981) recommended the use of term 'Adolescence

Education' in place of sex education and deliberately and consciously with a view to enhance its acceptability and facilitating the incorporation of suitable contents for this age group without destroying the traditional moralities and the innocence of adolescent boys and girls. National Youth Policy termed it 'Self Awareness Education'

Once such education is to be imparted this is to be remember that the teacher has to avoid both extremes of strict indoctrination and total relativism. At the same time, the teacher is expected to represent, and insist upon a central core of socially determined values to guide personal self-examination and decision making. This is a big challenge for the teachers and to meet this they have to be involved in themselves in personal examination and assessment in relation to ethics and values underlying interpersonal relationships. It is also desirable for them to have opportunities to become familiar with groups of adolescents and the development understanding and empathy with the problem which will emerge in the classroom. They are to be aware of students' eagerness for and receptivity to for information and guidance on matters of sex and sexuality and interpersonal relationships they have to dispel misinformation often prevalent in young people through various unreliable sources and to suggest the dangers of their actual ignorance about sex and sexuality.

Mehra (2000) observed that sexual and reproductive health programmes in country remains ineffective not only because they ignore the needs of adolescents who comprise about 30% of the population, but also because they fail to tackle the sexuality issue head-on on going programmes relating to reproductive health education, HIV/AIDS preventive education tend to tackle the issue sideways instead of hitting it directly.

Weis and Kataria (2000) have emphasized the need for research work in this area in western countries as well as India.

UNFPA (2000) has expressed its concern over the issues related to Adolescents and inadequate data available on the matter of sex and sexuality.

There is a need to look into the possibilities of making these programmes more successful and effective, programmes of such education can be meaningfully planned on the ground realities. Although various surveys provide some information on some of the sexuality issues which paint a scanty picture. Insight into the reality can be obtained by systematic research into the basic values and perceptions of those affected and affecting the educational process. So the present study has been undertaken to look into the values and perceptions of adolescent students and their teachers relating to sex and sexuality.

1.5 Statement of the Problem

The problem of the proposed investigation is to study: *"Values and Perceptions of Adolescent Students and Their Teachers relating to Sex and Sexuality".*

1.6 Terms Defined

Values : Values are those desires and goals accepted by the society which are internalised through the process of socialisation and which become subjective, preferences, standards and aspirations.

Perception :	Perception is the process by which a person interprets sensory stimuli. Perception is translation of these sensory images into understandable forms.
Sex and Sexuality Values :	Sex related values are those constructs which serve as internal and Perceptions guide for human sexual behaviour in its biological, psychological, socio-cultural and moral dimensions.
Sex :	Dictionary meaning of Sex is 'by which a plant or animal is male or female'. It indicates the differences in Morphology and Anatomy Morphology is which separates from male from female. Wrong perception by some members of society about sex is sexual intercourse, pregnancy, childbirth or the processes leading to them.
Sexuality :	Sexuality refers to enormous range of social and individual acts and attitudes that engage 'mind and body' in manifold and diverse ways. Sexuality takes different forms and meanings depending on one's gender, class or position. It is learnt socially.
Adolescence :	This stage is a transition between childhood and adulthood and relatively recent

		social inventions characterised by rapid physical and psychological changes, increasing personal autonomy from parents and family, social experimentation, idealism, conflict and personal uncertainty.
Early Adolescence	:	On set of puberty Female age – 8-12 years Male age – 10-14 years
Characteristics of Early Adolescence	:	▪ starts to move to peers ▪ vicillates between clinging and rebellion ▪ strives for independence ▪ may be confused, pre-occupied with body wonders 'am I normal?' ▪ may experiment with same sex or sexual behaviour ▪ begins to think abstractly
Middle Adolescence	:	Female age – 13-16 years Male age – 14-17 years
Characteristics of Middle Adolescence	:	continues efforts to establish separate identity from parents ▪ often becomes idealistic and altruistic ▪ interested in dating, exploring sex ▪ loves intensely, 'desperately' ▪ continues to develop abstract thinking
Late Adolescence	:	Female age – 16 and above Male age – 17 and above

Characteristics of Late Adolescence :	▪ declares independence ▪ establish a set body image ▪ loves more realistically, develops commitment ▪ peer group becomes less important, more detective of friends ▪ develops more consistent framework of values, moral ethics ▪ able to think abstractly ▪ defines life goals

1.7 Objectives of the Study

The objective of the present investigation is to study Sex and Sexuality Related Values and Perceptions of adolescent students and effect of sex and SES on them forming sixteen objectives in all as listed below:

1. To study the sex and sexuality related values and perceptions of teachers and their adolescent students.
2. To study the sex and sexuality related values and perceptions of male and female adolescent students.
3. To study the sex and sexuality related values and perceptions of adolescent students belonging to low, middle and high SES.
4. To study the sex and sexuality related values and perceptions of male and female students of low SES.
5. To study the sex and sexuality related values and perceptions of male and female students of middle SES.

6. To study the sex and sexuality related values and perceptions of male and female students of high SES.
7. To study the sex and sexuality related values and perceptions of males of low, middle and high SES.
8. To study the sex and sexuality related values and perceptions of females of low, middle and high SES.
9. To study the interactional effect of SES and sex on sex and sexuality related values and perceptions of students.
10. To study the sex and sexuality related values and perceptions of TGT and PGT grade teachers.
11. To study the sex and sexuality related values and perceptions of male belonging to TGT and PGT grades.
12. To study the sex and sexuality related values and perceptions of females belonging to TGT and PGT grades.
13. To study the sex and sexuality related values and perceptions of male and female of TGT grade.
14. To study the sex and sexuality related values and perceptions of male and female teachers of PGT grade.
15. To study the sex and sexuality related values and perceptions of male and female teachers.
16. To study the interactional effect of sex and being PGT or TGT on Sex and Sexuality Related Values and Perceptions of teachers.

1.8 Delimitations

Keeping in view the nature of the problem and research design and also the constraints of time and resources, the present study has been delimited in the following ways:

- The study has been conducted in NCT of Delhi only.
- Kendriya Vidyalayas located in Delhi were selected for the study.
- The students of class 10th, 11th and 12th were taken for the study.
- PGTs and TGTs teaching classes 10th, 11th and 12th formed the sample of teachers.

2

Review of the Related Theoretical and Research Literature

2.1 Introduction

In view of the necessity of inclusion of sex and sexuality related concepts into the curricula, this becomes essential that the curriculum in the area is developed, in the light of an over-burdened and heavy curriculum, through integrated approach and curriculum transactional strategies are devised accordingly. For such an exercise, the findings of various research studies of the field undertaken in India and abroad are reviewed and properly utilized.

The problem here is that education about sex and sexuality is a recent intervention as has been discussed in Chapter-I. Hence, not many studies in the area have been undertaken. Kataria (2000) rightly opines that the research is weak area in the field. Whatever studies related to the subject are available in India have been undertaken under the umbrella of population education/adolescence education. Even in abroad, not much has been done. Weis (2000) reports that current state of affairs in the researches on sexuality education in schools is dismal.

As the things are, not a good number of research studies are available. Some theoretical and research work has been done on education about sex and sexuality in the fields of population education. Only a few specific studies on the topic have been undertaken by research institutions, NGOs and media.

In the following part of the chapter, the theoretical literature and studies related to the topic have been reviewed under Section A and Section B respectively, in chronological order.

Section A

2.2 Indian Literature

2.2.1 Thoeretical Literature

Mehta, Saxena & Mukherjee (1969), have shown Pros and Cons of Sex Education within the population education topic and develops the arguments rather than simply dismissing the sex education factor as too controversial.

Rehman (1979), developed a Population education curriculum for out of school youth. One of the important areas of the curriculum is human reproduction, contraceptives and birth control devices.

Muley, D.S. et.al (1994), The National Seminar Report on Adolescence Education covers all its dimensions namely process of growing up, sex and sexuality, drug abuse and STD/HIV.

Bhatia & Chandra (1993), have reported in their article that WHO considers adolescence to be the period between 10 & 20 years during which individuals undergo significant psycho-sexual and psycho-social development. Adolescent pregnancies make upto 15% of the total and may be largely neither physically nor emotionally fit for pregnancy and motherhood. Adolescents who marry between the age of 15-19 have 6-7 children over the course of their lives. they suggested intervention programmes like education and health care for girls aged 10-15, use of contraception, and family life education.

Muley, D.S. & Others. (1994), The National Seminar report on Adolescence Education contains informative papers on different dimensions of adolescence education. It serves as a source material on adolescence education covering areas like the process of growing up, sex and sexuality, drug abuse and STD/AIDS.

Upmanya & Sushma (1994), are of the view that adolescent depression is a serious problem in India, as evidenced by the sharp rise in adolescent suicide, but data are lacking. The study examines depression among female and male India adolescent, in relation to sex role orientation.

ICPD: POA (1994), Action for the 21st Century reproductive health and rights contained in the ICPD programmes of action prepared by Family Care International includes sections on Women's empowerment and gender equity, eliminating discrimination against girls, males responsibility and participation; sexual and reproductive health rights including safe motherhood, unsafe abortion, adolescents, prevention and treatment of STDs/HIV/AIDs.

Nag (1994), is of the view that with no vaccine in sight for immunization against the AIDS – transmitted virus HIV, the only feasible method of controlling the spread of the disease seems to be through behavioural prevention. There is an urgent need for an awareness to be created among the people regarding those aspects of sexual behaviour which are particularly risky. Topics such as premarital sex, extra marital sex, female sex workers, homosexuals, male sex workers are covered by this paper. High risk behavioural involving the above aspects are common in India according to evidence and statistics presented

Kapoor, J. Mehta S. (1995), is of the opinion that the provision of sex education for adolescents is a taboo subject in India and essentially unavailable from any source. In India, sex is rarely discussed, even among married couples. Sex and marriage are viewed as synonymous, with strict segregation by sex among adolescents, especially in rural areas. CHETNA, a non-governmental organisation in Ahmedabad, began, holding sex education workshops in 1990 as part of residential health fairs or camps for adolescents. 150-200 adolescents aged 1-18 convene in a residential camp at a school or other sufficiently large facility for 3-4 days during which role playing, games, reading materials, and small group discussions are used to talk about physical and emotional changes in adolescence, love, sex, sexuality, and gender issues. While positive changes have been observed in many participants, it is clear that parental involvement is essential to sustain the gains made and to provide support.

Sankaran (1995), focusses on adolescent girls[1] need to get relevant information before sexual activity begins. According to the author young girls should be encouraged to develop their own values and attitudes towards sexuality at the same time difference in value and attitudes need to explored, respected and sympathised with. Discussion of values should not take place in abstract, but in relation to young girls own experience, expectation of sexual relationships and wider moral issues affecting their lives.

Kakodkar (1995), refuted the charges of promiscuity on sex education and term family life education has been recommended.

Kala (1995), expresses the view that Indian traditional value of one sexual married partner is of great value in the era of HIV/AIDS epidemic.

Those indulging in polygamy or many sexual partners are actually carriers of HIV for the woman at home.

Kalra & Kalra (1996), call for sensitivity in dealing with subjects related to sex and sexuality. It considers that main mode of transmission of AIDS in through sex, only 3% being through blood transfusion. Hence sex education is only hope to prevent AIDS.

The authors have dealt with adolescent and AIDS, teaching sexual health, clarification of values and AIDS, cultural heritage and sexual behaviour pattern in third world countries with special reference to India in their handbook on 'AIDS Education'.

Chugh (1998), Myths and misconceptions related to sex and sexuality are prevalent in society since ages. A glance at any agony column of newspaper and magazine gives evidence enough of the gross misinformation regarding sex. Some sexual myths are so prevalent that even educated men fall prey to it. Such sexual myths are: sex is most thing of our life, masturbation is abnormal and unhealthy, love and sex seen as synonymous, males have greater interest in sex, a few drinks before sex improve the quality of sex, intercourse is the endpoint of every sexual activity, age does not end sexual activity, women are affected much less by the process of ageing.

The Times of India (1998), reports that dating is normal for most of urban and semi-urban teenagers and society is also changing its attitude about meeting of a boy and girl outside home and school. Still some parents of middle class society show conservative attitude about dating and discussions on girl friend and dating issue are not so open.

The Times of India (1999), reports that youngsters are having sex sooner in relationships and this is despite being young in the times of AIDS where, just the health risks ought to slow them down.

Kalra & Kalra (1999), in the handbook 'Adolescent & AIDS' deal with AIDS and other subjects related to sex and sexuality. Main thrust areas of the handbook are: AIDS & Adolescents – the third world at risk, teaching sexual health, AIDS and its prevention, Clarification of values and AIDS, Cultural heritage and sexual behaviour, Psychic drugs, AIDS, Alcohol & Adolescents and healthy living.

Kuthalia Anjana (1999), finds a shift in values of faithfulness to life partner and towards more liberal attitudes of women. This phenomenon is very old for men in open and for women it has come more openly in recent times. She refers Khuswant Singh who opines that besides rape and breaking a promise, every relationship between a man and a woman is acceptable.

The Times of India (1999), reports that teenagers want more freedom to stay late night out and go to pubs and discos which may make some parents to worry about their well being. Concern of parents is justified for their children.

Chugh (1999), is of the view that suppressing the normal desires of an adolescent and making them submissive will greatly harm the emotional development of their personalities.

Rahul (1999), observes that ironically, teenagers subconsciously like limits to be imposed on them. This helps them ponder over their innate sense of rebellion. Sociologists believe that adolescents thrive on confrontation and feel wanted when some one is looking out for them. Psychologists say moderate intervention is perhaps the best approach while dealing with teenagers as adolescents are unpredictable. Limits should be set by a parent but with a supportive approach.

Walia N. (1999), observes that today's teenagers are more aware and critical savvy of the changes going on in society. Children do not approve of flirtations of fathers and skirt-clad mothers. They are their biggest critics.

Kanti Raj, K. (1999), emphasizes that use of condom is definitely a good precaution measure against HIV infection but one man – one woman norm, is the best bet against AIDS.

NCERT (2000), A learning package for adolescents has been prepared by the NCERT. In 1994, International conference on population and development exhorted all countries to protect and promote the right of adolescents to reproductive health information. First step has been taken in this direct realising that school curriculum has failed in this aim. A national consensus was evolved in 1993 but not much of headway could be achieved due to apprehensions of parents and educators. The package gives complete knowedge base, general framework of adolescent education, answer of commonly asked questions and activities tailored to integrate into curriculum.

Sekhon, Aradhika (2000), is of the view that thousands of people are going to be AIDS victim very soon. With 3.5 million people in India infected with the virus, the HIV infection has been labelled as an 'epidemic' in many developing countries like Africa, India and those in S.E. Asia. Though medical care is the basic step in combating the virus, awareness and support system are vital. The fact we need to face today is that sex education is not the main issue but AIDS is. A greater awareness about AIDS, be it related to drug abuse or sex, will result in more compassion and support for the

HIV positive people and their families.

The Times of India (2000), reports that men feel a crying need for sex education to dispel their myths about sex and women. Otherwise, they are forced to learn it from older boys and from films.

Since parent preach and do not give proper knowledge of sex to children due to social ethos and prudence.

Mehra (2000), observed that sexual and reproductive health programmes in country remain ineffective not only because they ignore the needs of adolescents who comprise about 30% of the population, but also because they fail to tackle the sexuality issue head-on. Ongoing programmes relating to reproductive health education, HIV/AIDS preventive education tend to tackle the issue side ways instead of hitting it directing.

Weis & Kataria (2000), have emphasized the need for research work in this area in western countries as well as India. There is a need to look into the possibilities of making these programmes more successful and effective, programmes of such types of education can be meaningfully planned on the ground realities. Although, various survey provide some information on some of the sexuality issues which paint a scanty picture. Insight into reality can be obtained by systematic research into the basic values and perceptions of those affected and affecting the educational process.

Sharma (2000), reported in her article that the new youth policy for India is disappointing as sex education and other important issues have been ignored in it by the Government. In our country we have children giving birth to children. We must realise that in the name of embarrassment if we do not tell our child, he will ask somebody else. This concept will be skewed.' In India, there are no programmes to cover the age of group of 10-15 years. This is the age when children form life long impressions and concepts we must not shun their inquisitiveness. Questions like teenage pregnancies, promiscuity were not addressed. Sex Education has been handled inadequately. Counsellors were not well-trained, stand had to be softened as parents also objected. Boys and girls were counselled separately for this reason. The policy framer agrees that India had a long way to go to reach the level of Thai Schools who have implemented the programme effectively.

Times of India (2000), Politicians oppose sex education in Madhya Pradesh while Government has ventured to extend the programme to 90 other schools in the next two months and opposition BJP steeped to condemn the decision. (pass a resolution against it) 'This cruel move will corrupt young minds' has been the opinion of Vipin Dixit.

Sangwan (2001), has reported in her article the trends evident in attitudes of teenagers today are extremely dangerous and well eventually lead to lumpenisation of society. She reported that peer pressures adolescents behave in a certain way which may be related to smoking, fashion or girl/boy friend. Sex education should be introduced to develop set of attitudes in the adolescents.

Kumar (2001), reported in the article that in nuclear families of today Television has acquired the status of the third parent. He has again that may lead to lowering the order of society. He also opined that they are disillusioned with the education system. The adolescents are busy in cementing their relationships which they should have been busy in their career building.

Nagpal (2001), reported in the article that today's adolescent was finding it difficult to postpone his/her desires. He further opined that sex is gratification and lust is being confused with love.

Almeida (2001), in his article opined that there are a number of cases in society who are 'homophobic' and they are uncomfortable on being around homosexuals.

2.2.2 Research Literature

Bhatwadekar & Israel's (1970), The objective of the study was to create a wholesome healthy attitude towards sex from childhood, to satisfy the needs of growing children, to help them through childhood and puberty and to correct the misconceptions and alleviate some of the common worries which may arise during physical development

Balasubramaniam et al. (1970), have studied high school teachers reactions to population education as integral part of the curriculum with the objective to find out whether teachers were in favour of teaching sex education along with population education. Sample consisted of 105 school teachers from 12 high schools located in Chembur – a northern suburb of Greater

Bombay selected randomly. Alongwith other findings, it was noted that majority of the teachers were of the opinion that sex education should be taught alongwith population education. They felt that it would help in removing wrong ideas and build up the moral character of students.

Pohlman, Edward & Rao (1970), undertook the study of the views of teachers on birth planning.

Sample consisted of 832 male and female (672 male and 160 female) teachers from elementary and secondary schools in rural and urban areas of Delhi & Haryana state.

Data collection was based on questionnaire and interview.

Findings indicated that there was a general agreement in both the interview and questionnaire data that the topics on 'overpopulation' and 'need for small families' should be introduced in the school curriculum, but they strongly disapproved of the inclusion of the topics on 'How a child is conceived'.

In another finding teachers opined that population education should be divorced from sex education.

Varghese (1970), studied the attitude of teachers towards different aspects of population problems, sex education and family planning.

Four point attitude scale was used for 276 teachers from primary and high school level form the city of Bangalore.

Findings showed that primary teachers and high school teachers differed in their attitude towards population education. Male and female teachers differed in their attitude towards population education. Marital status of teacher was not related to their attitude to sex education. Teachers belonging to different religions differed in their attitude to sex education.

Maheshwari (1972), undertook a study of the receptiveness of school teachers to population education. Objective was to study opinion of teachers towards the adoption of a small family norm and to find out the opinion of teachers regarding the ways and means of introducing population education in schools. Sample was 300 teachers (150 male and 150 female) from 28 Government schools of South Delhi.

Findings showed that teachers had very high awareness of the population problem that world is facing. 80 per cent teachers agreed that small family is advantageous leading to happy and comfortable life. Majority of teachers felt that adults should be educated in the philosophy of family planning. 83 per cent teachers agreed that anatomy and physiology of human reproduction should form a part of population education. These teachers were against introducing sex education in schools.

Patel (1973), conducted a study of knowledge and attitude towards human reproduction among XI standard students in some urban schools. Objectives of the study were to find out the information of students about the human reproduction system to understand the attitude of students towards sex education, to find out the sources of information for this knowledge and to find out the knowledge of students about contraceptive devices. Sample of the study was 50 students (32 boys and 18 girls) belonging to different caste groups in age of 14-19 years. A knowledge test containing 42 objective type questions were developed pertaining to human reproduction. A questionnaire was developed to find out their attitude to the introduction of sex education in schools.

Mehta (1974), studied the opinion of parents and teachers towards introduction of population education in high schools of Bhubaneshwar.

Main Objectives of the Study were

- to find out the opinion of teachers and parents towards the inclusion of certain contents of population education in high school curricula, to study the opinion of parents and teachers regarding the importance of population education in various spheres of social life, to study sex difference in the opinion expressed by the teachers and to study the opinion of parents belonging to different income groups and educational background.

Sample consisted of 100 teachers (50 males and 150 females) from different schools of Bhubaneshwar city. An opinionaire of 46 items was developed with a three-point scale.

Findings indicated that teachers and parents irrespective of their sex and educational background had a favourable opinion towards inclusion of population contents and process of human reproduction in the education programme. Parents and teachers both felt that agencies other than schools are more suitable to teaching of population education. Parents and teachers irrespective of sex difference or income and education background have expressed the opinion against the teaching of human reproduction in schools. However, teachers from high income group were more favourable inclined towards this view than group were strongly opposed to this opinion.

Nagda et al (1974), studied the opinion of teachers towards population education.

Objective of the study was to find out the existing knowledge and attitude of teachers towards population related problems. Sample consisted of 100 teachers of Chittor District. Sixty five percent felt that population education and family planning are one and the same.

25 per cent considered that population awareness and planned parenthood as a part of population education.

90 per cent felt that population education is necessary for the youth for responsible parenthood.

Most of the respondents felt that it is necessary to impart knowledge on human reproduction and nutrition to our masses.

Regarding the methodology to be adopted for creating population awareness among the community 50 per cent considered exhibitions and films show as appropriate methods where as 30 per cent considered lectures by experts group discussions as appropriate methods.

Patel (1974), conducted a study of population awareness of pupils of standard X at Varnama high school. Objective of the study was to find out awareness of students about population problems. Some of the findings are of interest as a good number of students considered late marriage as an advantage. In most cases, students did not discuss the personal problems with parents. Girls were more knowledgeable about family planning than boys.

Ramachandran (1974), studied the knowledge and attitude of teachers of Kurnool towards population education. An orientation training course in population education was arranged for teachers of SV University.

In pretest 40 per cent participants considered population awareness programme as a part of family planning propaganda. In final test 80 per cent of participants considered that population awareness is a part of population education. Before the course 60 per cent considered that family planning and population education were one and the same. But after the course most of the participants considered that family planning and population education are not one and the same. In post test most of them thought size of family can be controlled through awareness and other devices.

In pretest and post test there was agreement among the participants that sex education in context of population is necessary to eliminate some misconception about human reproduction in the younger generation.

Gupta (1974), studied the knowledge and attitude of teachers towards introduction of sex education in school curricula.

The objectives of the study were to find out whether teachers have adequate knowledge about sex education, to find out the attitude of teachers towards the introduction of sex education in schools, to find out whether there is any difference in the attitude of male and female teachers towards introduction of sex education in schools, to find out whether teachers belonging to rural-urban areas differ in their attitude towards sex education and to find out whether teachers belonging to different religious groups differ in their attitude towards the introduction of sex education in schools.

Sample consisted of 250 teachers belonging to different sex, religion were drawn from different types of schools of Bhopal, Indore and Ujjain, Div. of Madhya Pradesh. A knowledge test of 17 questions and attitude scale of 43 statement was developed.

A majority of teachers realised that sex education should necessarily form an integral part of the school education. Most teachers suggested that best to sex education was use of films. Contents of sex education recommended by teachers were:

- Health and hygiene
- Anatomy and physiology of reproductive organs
- Menstruation and seminal emissions
- Contraceptives

Teachers have suggested that sex education should be imparted along with teaching of subjects like Biology and Social Studies health and hygiene.

Majority of teachers opined that it should be taught be Biology teacher and some teachers preferred doctors.

Rao A.H.K. (1974), has studied the attitude of parents and teachers towards the introduction of sex education in secondary schools. Sample consisted of 300 teachers from 31 secondary schools and 300 parents from Mysore city. A questionnaire was used in the form of attitudinal statement.

Findings showed that there was no significant difference in the attitude of parents and teachers towards sex education. The teachers and parents both favoured the introduction of sex education in schools and recommended that scientific approach to the teaching of sex education should be followed. They felt that sex education is very crucial for the development of balanced personality of students.

Alosius (1974), studied the opinion of parents and adolescents towards the introduction of sex education in schools. Sample consisted of 110 adolescents students from different high schools of Bangalore and their parents included in the sample.

- Both the teachers and adolescents had a favourable attitude to the introduction of sex education in schools. Christian parents were better disposed to sex education than Hindu and Muslims

Gangrade (PE) (1975), undertook a research-cum-action study on population education for university youth. Sample consisted of students of undergraduate colleges of Delhi University.

An action programme of exhibition, film show, debate and lecture – all related to various facets of population education was developed for the students. Questionnaire and interview were taken of students, parents and teachers.

The students, parents and teachers were of the view that the action oriented programme in population education should have the following media component at the University stage. Seminar, exhibition, film show and lectures on sex education should be organized which aimed at the Reproductive System and the development of proper values about sex. Contents of population education at University stage shall comprise of the many topics of which human reproduction, family life and interpersonal relationship and basic values and qualities of life for human progress.

Desai et.al. (1979), for developing Population Education Curriculum conducted 12 experiments with Class VIII and IX students. Health and hygiene formed a part of the curriculum. One of the experiments conducted was changing values. After the experiments, it was found that the students had developed better concept of a happy family.

Tribhuvan University (1982), Curriculum Development Centre conducted survey on knowledge and attitude survey on population education. Sample consisted of 150 students from all levels and 50 university teachers.

Majority of teachers agreed that a course on population education should include sex education and family planning. The students recommended that sex education and family planning should form a part of population education course.

Manorama (1990), FPAI has opened first sex education, counselling, research training therapy centre (SECRT) in 1978. Now in Bombay, Bangalore, Jabalpur, Lucknow, Chennai, New Delhi and Rajkot. The SECRT centres exist to create awareness among people, especially young people, about sexuality, healthy relationship and family well-being. The centres main activity is sex education programmes in schools and colleges training and orientations in Human Sexuality, reproductive health and counselling for sexually related issues.

Verma (1990), In this research work there is evidence that the home is a potential source of alienation and it may have devastating effect on adolescents in terms of generating psychological, social and academic problems.

Murthy (1991), His study seeks to develop an understanding of awareness of sex, reproduction, family formation and family planning among the adolescent, umarried, rural girls of Chittoor District, Andhra Pradesh. A sample of 600 umarried rural girls belonging to Harijan,, Muslim and Caste Hindu families was identified on the basis of the multi-stage simple random sampling technique. A self-constructed interview schedule was used in the study. Statistical techniques such as percentages, chi-square, and regression analysis were utilized. The pubertal age of respondents was around 13 years. Caste Hindu girls had better and earlier perception of sex and reproduction as compared to other group.

George (1991), attempted to identify sex related problems of adolescents in the colleges of Kerala and their perception on sex education issues. One thousand four hundred and seventeen students (663 boys and 754 girls) enrolled in Kerala University and Mahatma Gandhi University served as the sample in the study. A self-made Questionnaire and Sex-related Problems Check-list were the main tools. Interviews were also conducted on a small sample. The collected data were treated with analysis of variance.

While the social problems experienced by the boys and girls were similar, the physical, physiological and psychological problems were different. The profile analysis of variance of sex-related problems was significant for boys and girls. Friends appearted to be the primary source of information concerning sex. Parents were found to be the least preferred. Adolescents had a good number of superstitious beliefs about sex.

Vatsa (1992), As per the findings of the study, majority (68.3 per cent) agrees that masturbation weakens a person and 42.68 per cent are of the view that discharge is precious and it is made of many drops of blood. The result shows the prevalence of myths among youth.

National Crime Records Bureau (1992), finds:

One rape every - 54 minutes

Molestation every - 26 minutes

Kidnapping/abduction every - 43 minutes

Eve teasing every - 51 minutes

One dowry death every - 1 hour 42 min.

Cruelty act every - 33 minutes

Criminal offence against women - every 7 min.

SECRT – FPAI (1992), conducted a survey of attitudes and perception of education urban youth to marriage and sex. Sample consisted of 3850 educated urban unmarried youth (boys and girls) between 15-29 years of age in selected areas in all four regions of the country where FPAI has SECRT centres.

The results indicate that the attitudes of young people in all the four regions towards marriage and sexuality are more or less the same. Contrary to the belief that great changes have occurred in the attitudes and sexual behaviour of urban youth, the survey indicates that the process of change from orthodox to liberal sexual behaviour has been slow despite the onslaught of the media and modernising influences. A welcome attitudinal change relating to equality between marriage partner is evident, particularly among males in terms of the right of the wife to work outside the house and to make the decisions to do so and supporting the unmarried girls in the event of an unwanted pregnancy. There is a positive attitude towards the female child and towards family planning.

The survey has been exploratory in nature and suggest an indepth survey, particularly of sexual practices among both urban and rural youth.

Some other findings of the study are:

- 70 per cent male and 74.5 per cent female educated urban unmarried youth consider companionship as the main reason for marrying and 50.7 per cent and 34 per cent consider sexual satisfaction as the reason.

- In case of a girl friend/self becoming pregnant, 42 per cent male and 32.8 per cent female opt for marrying the girl/boy, 18 per cent and 33.8 per cent for telling it to parents.
- 53.5 per cent males and 74.6 per cent females have a negative attitude towards pre-marital sex.

Chhabra (1992), is of the view that changing attitudes towards sex and reproduction are evidenced by the desire to understand their physiological, behaviourial, and social aspects. He commented that illicit relationships are condemned, at the same time adolescents get sexual messages from Television, movies and books. In India high moral codes consider adolescent sexuality and the resultant motherhood a disgrace. 100 unwed mainly rural girls who came for medical termination of pregnancy to the Mahatma Gandhi Institute of Medical Sciences, Sevagram. 88 per cent of the girls did not know the consequences of having sexual relations; 90 per cent did not know anything about contraceptives and 66 per cent had come in the second trimester. A prospective study of school girls about their knowledge of menstruation, reproductive, physiology and birth control methods showed that 75.1 per cent of girls lacked that knowledge. (87.6 per cent of rural girls, as compared to 62.6 per cent of urban girls). The knowledge sources were mainly literature and movies (77.93 per cent). Premarital sexual intimacy among unwed adolescents is widespread. Some girls seek pregnancy termination when it is no longer possible; in these instances, the infant is often abandoned or killed. Health education and sex education are needed, and various welfare programmes should reach impoverished and rural areas.

Drakshayani Devi. K.; Venkata Ramaiah P. (1994), conducted interviews with 65 females of 14-15 years old in Guntur District in Andhra Pradesh to know their knowledge and practices about menstruation. 43 girls knew it as a physiological process while 22 girls thought it to be a curse from God, or a sin and a disease respectively. 50 per cent were restricted from household work, taking part in religious activities, attending marriages and playing. It showed the prevalence of many myths and misconceptions relating to this simple biological phenomenon for which source of information is mother, grandmother, friend and sister.

These findings clearly show the need for sex education through several channels, eg. TV, school nurses, health personnel, compulsory sex education in school and knowledgeable parents.

Dahleez (1994), A study by the Population Foundation of India (PFI) involving adolescent focus group has found that sexual activity among adolescents is occuring at earlier ages. The focus groups were formed in Shimla, Delhi, Hyderabad and Bangalore. The aim of the study was to provide information relevant to Dahleez, a radio soap opera which is part of a communication effort to provide population education and coverage of adolescent sexuality issues. The soap opera was aired in Hindi for youth aged 11-19 years. Dahleez was formed after a PFI survey of 17,200 adolescents from rural and urban Uttar Pradesh, Rajasthan, and Haryana and Delhi. It uncovered a need for a structured, systematic, yet entertaining, communication approach to sex education. DAHLEEZ was broadcast across the entire Hindi, belt over Yuvavani Channel on 30 stations of AIR. About 11,000 listeners were enrolled, of which 4,000 were sent a questionnaire after 26 episodes. The findings indicated that boys considered the ideal marriage age for girls to be 16 years and 20 years for boys. Girls thought marriage age should be 20 years for girls and 24 years for boys.

Maitra et.al. (1994), conducted a survey on Adolescent Sexuality education and sources of information.

A survey of 959 young females (ages 10-21 years) from India highlighted the importance of education attainment to fertility-related behaviours. Respondents represented a spectrum of educational levels: school drop-outs (32 per cent, primary and secondary school attendees, 84 per cent of them wanted to defer childbearing for at least two years after marriage. The desire for formal sex education was strong in all educational subgroups (about 62 per cent), however. It has been estimated that postponement of the marriage age from 16 years 20-21 years would result in a 20-30 per cent decrease in the annual number of births in India. School-based sex education represents a feasible mechanism for help to achieve this goal.

Marg – India Today Survey (1994), Surveys mostly on urban educated youth place high value on virginity. But indications are that there is a gradual change in behaviour and attitudes. Values of virginity, chastity, sexual fidelity, monogamy have been hailed against that premarital sex continues to be accepted by a large percent of youth. A certain percentage specially in metro cities have accepted western life styles and behaviours.

Yadav (1995), studied teenage fertility of rural females in eastern Uttar Pradesh. The findings suggest that marriage age is not likely to increase significantly in the near future. A number of socio-cultural constraints are at play that inhibit the increase in marriage age. Daughters are considered other people's wealth (paraya dhan) who have to be married off as early as possible to be rid of the burden of dowry. Illiteracy or low educational status and domestic work as the main occupation also promote lower marriage age.

Bansal (1995), had undertaken a study that was conducted at Transport Nagar in Indore, 210 such adolescents were surveyed by random sampling source of findings related to their sexual activity are 25.2 per cent of the cleaners had a history of sexual activity, commonly with prostitutes. In many cases payment to the prostitute was financed by the Senior Driver. 94.3 per cent of these adolescents had engaged in unprotected sexual intercourse and remaining 5.7 per cent had used condoms infrequently 98.5 per cent of them had not heard of HIV & AIDS. 4.3 per cent had a history of sexually transmitted diseases and had been treated by general practitioners. Special programmes are required for these adolescents to education them about the risks of unprotected sex and drugs in order to prevent them for contracting HIV/AIDS.

Bhattacharya and Joshi (1995), are of the view that early marriage was perpetuated in the past by tradition, beliefs about preservation of a girls chastity and female needs to reduce expenditure. Early marriage is still practiced in northern states of India, where the educational level of the girls is low. Premarital sexual relations are becoming more common, due to a relaxation of social and cultural norms restricting sexual behaviour. An Indian family planning survey found that 13% of girls and 28% of boys approved of premarital sexual relations. There appears to be an increase in adolescent abortion and post abortion on complication. The authors suggest that teachers and parents need to speak more honestly about sexual matters and that sex and health education need to be more effective.

Gupta and Khan (1995), conducted a baseline survey in Uttar Pradesh. Major recommendations of the study are related to premarital counselling for teenagers for delayed marriage and child bearing; media use for communicating this message; and role of literacy in postponing marriage, spacing births, family life education in the school curriculum and access to contraceptives.

Kapoor and Aditi (1996), The comprehensive survey conducted by Kapoor of 340 students aged 15-

20 years reveals that young's are highly conscious of the nuances of various programmes their content and format. The survey showed that teenagers overwhelmingly favour realistic balanced and informative programmes over those which are vulgar, irresponsible and artificial. Media provides healthy ground to discuss both positive and negative aspects of the sensitive subjects. It brings out the rational aspect of some of otherwise emotional issues.

Though the negative effect of media on teenager with impressionable minds has come in for sharp criticism, the voice of the victimised youth has hardly been heard.

IMRB-Survey (1997), The survey was conducted to ascertain the utility of imparting sex education in schools of nine metro cities. Opinion of younger and older generation was sought. 47 per cent-80 per cent younger people opined that it is good for schools to impart sex education while the percentage for older people was from 45 per cent to 81 per cent.

Arora, S. (1997), The present study was conducted with an aim of educating the school going adolescents about AIDS through a comprehensive AIDS awareness education programme and also determine its impact on their knowledge, attitudes and beliefs about AIDS and sexuality.

All the adolescents studying in standards IX and X of four schools were taken as the sample for the study. The total sample consisted of 300 adolescents in the age range of 13-16 years, of which 200 were female and 100 were males. Tools used to collect data included attitude scale, questionnaires, focussed group interviews and personal interviews and participatory as well as non-participatory observations. The statistical analysis included frequency, percentages, mean, SD and 'T' test.

The major findings of the study are: there was a considerable lack of awareness among the adolescents about AIDS and sexuality, specially the female adolescents before the implementation of AAEP and the AAEP had a significant positive impact. There was an overall gain in knowledge scores with greater increase among girls. The score enhancement was 88% for girls and 87 per cent for boys.

IIPS (1997), reports on the basis of a survey that among those who had heard about AIDS from more than one source. Most common source was Television (48 per cent), Newspaper (35 per cent) and radio 31 per cent less frequent were magazine (18 per cent) friends and relatives (10 per cent) school teachers were mentioned least.

The Times of India (1998), The report of 'The Times of India' dated 15 August that Indian youth is uncomfortable with homosexuality. Attitudes ranged from strong disapproval to being open-minded about this 66 per cent disapproved of any of their friends being homosexual. Calcutta and Chennai youth considered it to be perverted and abnormal.

The Times of India (1998), reports that girls should be given total freedom like boys. Nowadays parents want girls to be financially independent before marriage. Girls who are not financially independent suffer later, is the opinion of youth in TOI-Colgate-IMRB Poll showing a shift in values of working women and financial independence.

TOI – Colgate – IMRB Poll (1998), The survey report consists of two parts quantitative and qualitative. Methodology consisted of face-to-face interviews conducted with 2826 people in 10 metro cities. Age group was 18-26 years. Unmarried and married belonging to all socio-economic statuses.

The major findings of the survey are:

- The barriers in pre-marital sex as visualised by males and females are fear of aids: 65 per cent and 54 per cent, morally wrong 57 per cent and 69 per cent, respectively not accepted in family/society 50 per cent and 54 per cent, fear of pregnancy 33 per cent and 32 per cent.
- 45 per cent youth in India want to socialize with people of their choice, 42 per cent want sexual freedom, 48 per cent want freedom for social/family restrictions.
- 4 per cent youth would like to marry someone of own choice without parents' consent and 41 per cent of own choice with parents' consent.

The Times of India (1999), In the report "No sex education please, we are Indians.", various views ranged from in favour of sex education to opposed views by the children and adolescents – the responders were from all over Delhi.

The survey conducted by NIE came out with opinions like: if spreading of correct and necessary information is wrong then sex education is wrong, concept of sex education is not new to India, Khujraho temples or Ajanta caves were carved to educate about sex, sex is a matter of one's personal conduct it is like any other human instinct which can be satisfied like animals and sex education hardly helps. Even the modern countries who have adopted sex education from last three decades show no decline in any early sex related problems, that we propose to discuss through sex education, sex education is a must, because it does not mean teaching us about the act of making love but about the problems and queries of growing up. It would clear all myths and doubts related to this subject and help Indians control its growing population, teaching sex in public, the way it happens in the west - destroys the very essence of our culture.

Walia (2000), stated that AIDS cases are increasing in Delhi and out of 376 cases 121 have already died. The article also emphasised the need of greater awareness and preventive measures. 85% of HIV cases are from 'unprotected sex' and knowledge about the disease is the only way for its prevention. Using condom, faithfulness to one's married partner and abstinence are the ways to keep AIDS away.

Hindustan Times (2000), reports the trend of decreasing age of first sexual exposure. 53% females have first pregnancy before 18 years of age. Problem is more serious in developed countries where 15-19 years females figureing 1 Crore 40 lakhs because mother of which more than 50 per cent are unmarried. Indian and

Pakistan have 5 per cent adolescent married using use contraceptives while figure for Indonesia and Thailand in 90 per cent.

Times of India (2000), Politicians oppose sex education in Madhya Pradesh while Government has ventured to extend the programme to 90 other schools in the next two months and opposition BJP steeped to condemn the decision. (pass a resolution against it) 'This cruel move will corrupt young minds' has been the opinion of Vipin Dixit.

National Herald (2002), reported the Conference on Adolescent Health. It emphasized that programmes for adolescents should focus not only on issues like counselling services, contraception, nutrition and rehabilitation but also provide for other enabling factors such as life skills, developments and protection from abuse. As per the latest population projections of the Technical Group constituted by the Planning Commission, 22.8% or 230 million Indians are in the adolescent age group 10-19 years. This large group represents a major potential human resource and so addressing its needs would contribute significantly to economic development as well as societal concerns like gender parity, population stabilization, efforts and improved quality of life.

Despite prevailing laws which specifies the age of marriage for girls as 18 years, cultural pressures force parents to marry off their daughters at relatively early ages. In 1996, an average of 38 per cent of girls in the age group 15-19 years were married and the rate is much higher in rural areas. As a result of early marriage fertility in the adolescent age group is relatively high and this was all the more distressing as adolescence is physiologically immature for purpose of reproduction.

The Conference was organised by the World Bank aided India Population Projcct (IPP VIII) being implemented by Municipal Corporation of Delhi and the Department of Paediatrics, Hindu Rao Hospital. It was emphasised that adolescent age-group had limited knowledge about sexual and reproductive health. "A major area of concern is the emerging threat of HIV/ AIDS and the relative absence of information regarding these and other issues related to reproductive health has grave consequences for the country.

National Population Policy recognizes adolescents as under served category and aims to provide for their nutritional contraceptive and information needs, programmes for adolescent health must recognise the vast diversity existing in this segment of the population. Adolescents include a wide spectrum of category like those in school and out of school, working adolescents, sexually exploited children, married and unmarried, in tribal/rural/urban areas in institutions and those disabled in conflicts. Any programme for adolescents must necessarily address a multitude of such issues. The conference was aiming to sensitize the medical community which ironically remains largely ignorant of the special needs of adolescents.

National Herald (2002), In an article "Violence against girls on rise" published a report of the study titled 'Bharat mein Balika: Dharam,

Himsa, Chhamta Evam Parivartan' by child rights activists and Director of Centre of Concern for Child Labour, revealed that 'stripping' and 'acid throwing' were being used as the 'most effective way' to silence the girl who protest against sexual harrassment. "It is the easiest and the most effective way to humiliate a family, a community and a nation". Stripping or raping have become increasingly common in tenancy disputes, especially in Kolkata, the report pointed out and said that on an average, every thana records about ten cases of stripping a month. "This when 70 per cent of the cases go unreported.

The report based on a three-year study in 18 states encompassing field work of nearly 70 NGOs, interviewing 11,500 girls of the age group 6-18 and covering the role of religion, violence, opportunities and changes with regard to development of girls, pointed out that stripping, which is an organised and deliberate crime, has been clubbed with offences like sexual harrassment under the term "outraging a women's modesty' the maximum punishment for which was just two years imprisonment with or without fine. Stripping, the worst offence to a girl's fundamental right to live with dignity, often drive them to commit suicide, the report said and pointed out that by trivialising the crime the state colludes with criminals rather than protects the victims. "Low priority given by official hierarchy, minimal staffing and inadequate infrastructure they are provided with paucity of appropriate orientation, training and support system for those who run them and consequent lack of sensitivity of the system to the needs of girls in distress make the matters worse".

Though domestic violence against girls is widespread, it was difficult to get any data on this issue due to the institution of family enjoying undeserved immunity from public inquiry and scrutiny. Figures in police record are inadequate as these reported cases provide little insight into real nature of crimes against adolescent girls.

Domestic violence cut across class, community and education and is not only inimical to girls physical and mental health but often become life-threatening. However, inspite of violence being widespread very few institutors or NGOs provide emotional support, legal assistance and shelter to girl victims of violence, the report pointed out and said there was no national methodical effort for trauma treatment of girls who were victims of rape, molestation or other kinds of violence.

The juvenile justice system was not only insensitive to the emotional needs of girls. But its very structure was inadequate and often girls were maltreated and sexually abused in remand homes run by government departments.

Besides, girls in rural areas lack any kind of support system that their counterparts in urban areas enjoy as all the available structures and services for girls in distress were concentrated in cities and traditional adjucantion in village were often biased against girls.

Participation of girls in labour market was increasing faster than boys and nearly one million girls of below 18 years of age were engaged as maid servants in Indeia which was still an "invisible work".

The proportion of girls enrollng and completing their primary education remains little more than half that of boys. Moreover, social developments resulting from globalisation, liberalisation and terrorism have adversely affected girls' education and chances of training in states like Kashmir, Triputa, Meghalaya, Manipur, Assam Mizoram, Nagaland and parts of Andhra Pradesh and Bihar. Growing religious intolerance was also showing on their dress code and freedom for movement.

Despite the increasing economic growth, recent trends suggest a slowing down in urban areas of six northern states of Uttar Pradesh, Bihar, Madhya Pradesh, Rajasthan, Orissa and Assam in the programme towards reducing avaoidable infant deaths among girls, the report pointed out and said that much needed to be done to reduce malnutrition among girls in the country which was the highest in the world. It also recommended a national policy on adolescent girl.

Sex determination has staged a comeback in Punjab, Delhi, Maharastra and Haryana and was spreading to newer areas of Andhra Pradesh, Gujarat, Rajasthan and Madhya Pradesh, the report said.

Besides, girls suffering from reproductive track infection and other health problems do not get adequate medical treatment due to general negative attitude of the society and social stigma, male orientation of health services and lack of privacy for girls and their low status. Essential health care package for girls of puberty age and adolescence should be introduced in the national health policy.

Section B

2.3 Foreign Literature

2.3.1 Theoretical Literature

Crow & Crow (1965), Adolescent development and adjustment in personal and social context has been discussed in depth in this book. The book deals with biological and cultural bases of adolescent behaviour, interest and environment factors that serve as motivators of adolescents attitude and behaviour, including those of the developing sex urge, adolescent deviations, adolescents personal, religious and moral values, conflicts and behaviour disorders and the problems that adolescents meet in their family, school, vocation and social living. Even though few adolescents experience major crises in these areas, many of them encounter numerous minor thwartings, frustations, or conflicts.

Myrdal (1968), discusses logical relationship of sex education marital and parental education, and population policy. It is a document of social realities compelling population commission to advocate parenthood and family life education.

Mclary, Jamesleslie (1973), Mclary's book "Human Sexuality Physiological, Psychological and Sociological Factors, explored physiological, psychological and sociological factors in human sexuality. It identified human sexuality as a deep and meaningful relationships rather than the more fulfillment of a biological function. It enables the reader to better understand and accept his or her own sexual needs and behaviour, as well as of these of differing views and conduct. It is also covers legal and medical aspects of sexuality.

Sebald, Hans (1984), The book "Adolescence: A Social Psychological Analysis". discusses adolescence as an individual as well as a collective phenomenon. On the individual level the focus is on the adolescents reaction to the urban industrial conditions that have created an environment in which social roots are certain and personal identity in vulnerable. On the collective levels, the focus is on adolescents attempts to compensate for uncertainty and vulnerability by engaging in subcultures or even counter cultural behaviour on both levels.

Ministry of Education, Culture and Sports. Human Sexuality and Reproduction, Manila (1984), developed a module in population education for elementary and secondary school teachers.

The module gives due importance to the understanding of the nature of human sexuality and physiology of human reproduction. This understanding can develop a healthy attitude towards sex and lead to desirable sexual behaviour factor which are important in the acceptance and practice of fertility control.

Sexuality the document defined "as a quality of maleness or femaleness that determines the anatomy, behaviour, characteristics and personality of the individuals through which he is able to procreate or have children, which determines his relationship with other individuals and groups."

Ministry of Education, Culture and Sports, Manila (1984), emphasized the need to develop wholesome attitude towards sex and viable moral standard with respect to sexual behaviour.

Collins, Gary & others (1986), The book "Becoming the Best You Can Be" talks about the changes, the surprises, the dreams and joys of growing up in the teenage years. It has seven sections devoted to various themes. and is a guide for the adolescents to make them better adjusted persons with their body, mind and society at large.

Planned Parenthood Federation of America (1986), in the book "How to Talk with Your Child about Sexuality", recommended that the earlier parents start, the easier it will be for parents to be primary sexuality educators of their children and also to protect children from sexual abuse and how to deal when a child has been abused or raped. It also explains how community, family and cultural values are related to personal beliefs.

Yang Hsiu (1988), has examined the causes which have led to changes in our attitude towards sex and the relaxation of sexual moral controls. The study revealed that popular movies, TV Films, novels, magazines and commercial advertisements have created such an atmosphere which appears to encourage sex and giving young people an impression that there is nothing wrong with these new sex attitudes and recommended that marriage and sex have to be delayed till one starts earning. It also noted that influence of religion has declined with the increasing knowledge and science and technology. The fear of divine wrath in the matter of sex is diminishing fast. New ways of preventing pregnancy and contraceptives and their free availability has promoted sexual behaviour. Better communication and transport facility has helped to go for courtings. Knowledge of sex psychology and psycho-analytical principles has given intellectual respectability to sex. Early physical maturation and resultant sex urges are achieved much earlier than social maturity, economic independence and security.

Fathalla, Mohmud F. & Others (1990), A complete chapter in the volume has been focussed on growing problems related to adolescents sexuality and pregnancy, sexually transmitted diseases and human immuno deficiency virus.

Abramson (1990) noted that, as sexually related issues demanded urgent understanding and action, it became increasingly important to have an established corpus from which to draw. However, the quantitative measurement of sexual behaviour he recommended carried the risk of treating aspects of sexuality as a social or medical problem although ignoring the meaning and importance of sexuality in people's lives. He acknowledged, finally that sexual science must encourage a wide variety of research methods, including narrative and qualitative assessment and theoretical strategies as "the rarified and neutral viewpoint of a science". Abramson's view was useful at the time to bridge the chasm between researchers mapping epidemiological patterns and those more interested in the meanings of the behaviours under investigation.

Qualitative methods have a place in establishing a foundation of knowledge from which other kinds of scientific endeavours may depart. He finally acknowledges that sexual science must encourage a wide variety of research methods including narrative and qualitative assessment and theoretical strategies although nonetheless cautioning that sex researchers remembers "science" is defined by its methods. He warns that if sexual science is to be perceived as a legitimate science, it must use methods that are generally deemed scientific. Qualitative methods are useful in exploring "sexual variables" that are not easily counted and physiologically measured. Social Science may learn more if it draws from anthropological and sociological ways of studying and understanding the world.

Moore and Rosenthal (1991), seemed to assume that gay youth have more in common with middle-aged gay men than with other youth; lesbians were not even worthy of note. Must research with gay youth has focused on runaways and other troubled youth, but little research has been conducted with young gay people without such complicated problems. Young gay men, lesbians, bisexuals may have more in common with heterosexuals of their age and gender than with their older counterparts. Information about bisexuals is especially unknowledge and problematic because of the secrecy involved and the risk that clandestine behaviour poses to uninformed partners. Straight women and lesbians might be expected to be less likely to want to have sex with bisexual men and women, respectively, because of the risk of infection from men, contradicting a common representation of women as reservoir. This study explored the notion that men and women have more in common by sex than by sexual orientation, that gender has stronger influence on sexual behaviour and ability to negotiate sexually than sexual orientation.

Trock (1992), has studied sexual behaviour of adolescents in California. He has opined that when normative changes occur in the area of premarital sex, sexual behaviours are likely to change first, followed by changes in sexual attitudes, and finally leading to changes in interpersonal, psychological variables. If so, we now appear to be between the second and third stage of this "sexual revolution". During the next phase of "consolidation" we can expect to see movement toward uniformity of the sexes on various interpersonal psychological dimensions as they relate to premarital sexual relations. Social behaviour may have an impact on both gender roles and sexality and little else has by forcing men to be more expressive and women to be more assertive.

Sexual behaviours that put adolescence at risk for HIV infection are common among adolescents. By the time they are 17 years old, approximately 60 per cent of youth in Canada, the United States, and Australisa have sexual intercourse, usually without condoms or knowledge of each other HIV serostatus. Only one third of sexually active teenagers uses contraception consistently as reported by sexual census data for Northern California Contra Costa Country. In her random sample of 1000 adults, she found the age of sexual debut for those aged 18 to 24 years was slightly past 15 years. It is a truism that teenagers tend to feel invulnerable making a future risk of AIDS appear remote. Decisions are thus based on very tangible factors rather than on long term probabilities.

World Health Organisation (1993), The book written for WHO gives an overview of the current health situation of young people. It discusses the strengths and weaknesses of traditional responses to their needs, and suggest ways in which they can be improved.

Burton & Arbutnot (1993), Homo sexuality has been recognised in Ancient India Vatsayanan's 'Kama Sutra' refers to it as practice of oral sex by eunuchs with their male partners and by male servants with their masters. In western world both male and female (lesbians) are classified as 'gay'. In modern times, it usually refers to persons whose predominant erotic inclination is towards their own sex whether or not they engage themselves in homosexual behaviour.

Kasun (1994), argued that there is a direct relationship between the provisions of sex education and school based family planning in United States and premarital sexual activity and adolescent pregnancy. She states that after almost three decades of experience and study, the promoters of Government birth control, have failed to produce any evidence of its salutory effects. On the contrary the weight of the evidence, much of it published by its own proponents, shows it to be associated with increase in premarital sex, teenage pregnancy births out of wedlock, welfare dependency and abortions.

Advocates for Youth (1994), Information included in this report was gathered primarily from an invitational meeting of youth serving professionals convened in November, 1992. The report identifies major challenges in educating young people in small communities about HIV and other issues related to sexuality. It also details several strategies for overcoming barriers to HIV prevention and sexual education.

George (1994), In his article 'Sexual Morality' based on catechism of catholic church and Kieran Sawyer's book 'Sex & the Teenagers', he considers that one of the major factors contributing to prevention of AIDS is the issue of sexual morality. He discusses about the creation of male and female by God, chastity, offences against chastity and homosexuality. Further, he has given his lucid views about teenage sex, real love, safe sex, contraceptives and purification of the heart.

Safe Motherhood (1995), International Centre for Research on Women (ICRW) investigated factors which affect the nutritional status of adolescents girls in Benin, Cameroon, Ecuador, Guatemala, India, Jamaica, Mexico, Nepal and Philippines. Based on various findings ICRW has proposed four strategies for postponing first briths among female adolescents: encouraging later marriage providing family planning and reproductive health. Services specially for adolescents, providing family life education about options for the future and increasing educational opportunities.

Mc Coy, Kathleen (1995), recommended talking with the teenagers about birth control measures. Teenagers do have ideas about sex and despite of values and wishes he or she makes a choice them they should know how to prevent an unplanned pregnancy which could turn an unwise choice into a life of hardship, even tragedy. Facts and values presented in a proper manner can help teens to make wise choices.

Family Planning Association of Hong Kong. (1995), The handbook on 'Family Life Education' is for teachers who are interested in providing sex education to students at all levels. It relates new insight on youth peer relations; on the relationship between young people and family; on attitudes towards pornography; on sexual offenses; on HDs & STDs; and on the importance of family planning.

Rowe (1996), has expressed that behavioural research is needed to help explore and explain sexual behaviour in ways that can influence behaviour change and policy. By situating behavioural data within a wider social and cultural context qualitative research can potentially offer an important framework for the comparative analysis of data on sexual conduct. Whether carried out in conjunction with quatitative survey research or developed as an end in and of itself, a constructivist approach provides a depth of knowledge and understanding that will ultimately be necessary to develop more effective responses to the risk posed by AIDS. Qualitative methods can contribute to the creation of language that articulate what we are trying to assess. Anthropology has long been concerned with the study of identifying valid category terms within a culture, and we can use that knowledge to develop qualitative methods that will work for public health.

Survey data will lack validity if such research does not precede it. Most surveys have taken the form of knowledge, attitude, and practice (KAP) questionnaires, which have methodological problems with assessments of sexual practice and unsafe sex. Researchers who do not take into account respondents' knowledge of their partners' sexual history and HIV antibody status and their meaning for sexual actors may incorrectly categorize all unprotected intercourse as risky behaviour.

Ryan & Cooper (1996), opine that girls are under represented in career and jobs. Teachers often communicate their different expectations for boys and girls to their students. Boys enjoy more attention at school and home. This difference in social treatment is responsible for different set of values and attitudes in both sexes.

The author further opined that In the past, sexual behaviour was considered an area where a community had a complete right to impose its standards on those people selected to teach its children and expected them to pass to young the community's positive values. Currently, however, the courts are viewing teacher's private sexual habits or preferences as separate from their public, professional lives as teachers.

In 1969, California Supreme Court ruled in a homosexual teacher Morrison's favour. The court acknowledged that homosexuality is an uncertain or controversial area of morality. Personal sexual life should not be affecting his relationship with his students or in any way affecting the performance of his teaching duties or, infact, affected his relationship with his fellow teachers. Court in general are allowing teachers a good degree of freedom in their private and personal life styles, as long as their choices and their behaviour do not adversely affect their performance as teachers.

Wieland, Sandra (1997), 'Hearing the Internal Trauma' that offers the rapists an innovative clinical model for understanding what happens within a sexually abused child. Combining the latest research findings in child development, early attachment, sexual abuse and trauma with extensive clinical experience, this clearly written book assists therapists in not only recognising signs of a child or adolescents abuse but also developing effective therapeutic interventions. Down the ages victim has been specially women who has to bear social and mental agony. Newspapers report such crimes with their commercial interests sometimes. According to Times of India 3 per cent of such crimes are reported of which very few get punishment.

Kirby & Wilcox (1997), are of the view that 'abstinence only' shape as approved by US congress should be 'abstinence based' i.e. to offer information about safer sex techniques and contraceptives in the event that adolescents do not choose abstinence. What was once a moral issue is clearly a public health issue.

Lear (1996), has discussed about social constructivist approaches and the study of sexuality. Various tensions continue among approaches to sexual health between public health and the biological sciences, between epidemiology and health promotion, between research and intervention, between quantitative and qualitative methods. Research on the transmission dynamics of HIV has helped to legitimize the study of sexual behaviour and contributed to a dialogue on the nature of good science, the purpose of research in public health, and the appropriate methods for studying sexuality. AIDS was prsented and claimed by the biomedical model, and it was this model that has largely defined the discourse of the epidemic. Though biomedical perspectives on sexuality have been and continue to be contested by the post-modernists and constructivists, feminists and queer thoerists, the very fact that they challenge the hegemonic position denotes their historically less privileged stance in the debate. Within a public health perspective, these challenges offer valuable balance between examining sexual practice and exploring its meaning to sexual partners; hence, this work sits somewhat uneasily between positivist and postmodern perspectives as an interactionist approach framed by a feminist perspective.

Public health was not only the field of study unprepared to deal with HIV. Even anthropology, with its claim to categorizing sexual customs and mores, was reluctant to regard sexuality as a legitimate subject of study until the early 1990s. She stressed the importance of an understanding of the meaningful context in which sexual behaviour takes place and the subjective meaning that this interaction invests in such behaviour for individuals. By focussing on meaning, it is possible to address a range of issues related to the significance of sexual behaviour, its erotic and social values, what makes a particular sex act or partnership satisfying, its psychological impact, and so on. Nuanced understandings of the meanings associated with sexual behaviour, with criteria for partner selection and notions of desire and pleasure, have only recently become a focus of research in relation to HIV and should also be applied to other situations of sexual risk, such as sexually transmitted diseases and coercive sexual encounters. This understanding is critical to translate social and behavioural research findings into more effective prevention strategies. Interpretive interactionism, based on symbolic interactionism, offers a useful theoretical framework with which to explore sexual issues.

Lear (1998), has dealt in detail with Sexual Culture and Sexuality in the present era. Like previous epidemics, HIV is historically situated, confronting global social and cultural systems and posing problems that must be integrated with extant notions of health and sexuality. Like other epidemics, AIDS is more than medical phenomenon. Although its general prevalence among youth in industrialized countries such as United States, Canada, the United Kingdom and Australia, remains relatively low, its sympolic significance is high. Changing risky behaviour because of fear or threat of HIV reduces risk of more common sexually and intravenously transmitted diseases, such as chlamydia, syphilis, and hepatitis. Initiating dialogue among young people about acknowledging desire, the right to request or refuse sex, and negotiating sex can be a positive social effect of HIV prevention programs.

After briefly discussing the study of sexuality, which follows, Chapter 2 begins by discussing the application of a critical interactionist perspective to the study of sexuality. Chapter 3 through 6 continues with the interview results, the methodological focus of this research. Finally, Chapter 7 discusses the findings and their implications for health education research and practice.

Sadiq Nafis (2000), in her article 'A Few Thoughts for the New Century' calls for universal access to information and services to promote women's right to reproductive health and protection, against harmful traditional practices. There is a need to build male attitudes and society at large to end violence against women.

UNESCO (2000), observes that in Indian society it is more or less of an ideal teacher on who's shoulder another responsibility of adolescent and sex education has fallen. In the wake of present situations of epidemic of AIDS where parents are failing to sex socialise their children.

Students are confiding in their teachers for better guidance and knowledge.

Weis & Carbonell (2000), explored race and gender work done under the auspices of an abstinence based sex education programme in an urban magnet school. While it was generally acknowledged that there was not nearly enough sexuality education in schools that while existed leaves much to be desired. In these curricula young men are painted as biologically programmed sexual aggressors while women are scripted as passive victims whose only subject position was that of not provoking easily sexually aroused males. Research showed that compulsory heterosexuality was inscribed throughout the school curriculum. The author comments that most states have developed sex education curricula and guidelines that were minimal and inadequate. One third of such material included reference to abstinence only. Discussion of sexual behaviour, when included tended to focus on negative consequences of sexual activity. Potentially controversial topics such as sexual orientations, abortion, masturbation and shared sexual behaviour were rarely covered. Few States required the sex education teacher to have certification or receive training in Sex Education.

2.3.2 Research Literature

Ministry of Education, Culture and Sports, Manila (1973), conducted a study of reactions of Parents and Teachers to potentially controversial topics in population education.

Objectives of the study were to determine

specific groups of parents and teachers who register opposition. Other objective was to solicit suggestions on the appropriate age/grade/ year level, when to introduce & how to teach the controversial topics. Sample of the study were two representative provinces and one city from each of the 12 regional divisions. The total sample of 6,644 respondents. 2093 parents (570 males and 1623 females). 2,441 elementary school teachers (420 males and 2021 females) and 2,110 secondary school teachers (668 males & 1442 females) Data was collected through interview and discussion using an open ended questionnaire.

Majority of parents favoured the inclusion of the controversial topics in the school curricula. 89.3 per cent favoured naming and showing the different contraceptive devices. In the order of their frequency, the reasons given for the objections as given by parents and teachers are as follows:

- School children are too young to know and mention the sex organs and the reproductive process (44.03 per cent)
- Sex is ugly and obscene (24.84 per cent)
- School children may become immoral and indulge in sex activities at an early age (8.59 per cent)
- School children may get married at an early age (8.59 per cent)
- It is unnecessary to teach sex education to children, since they already know about it (4.24 per cent)

About 50 per cent of the elementary school teachers and one third of the parents and secondary school teachers suggested that the topics related to sex be taught starting in grade I. Family size norms and abortions may be covered in first year of high school.

Lee (1975), studied relationships between specialisation and attitude towards population related issue among professional students in Korea. Objective of the study were to determine whether students in health professions in general are more likely to show positive attitude towards family planning, abortion and population education than students in the teaching profession value larger families more than students in the health profession. Sample consisted of all the students enrolled in teacher's college, the Medical College and department of nursing. 1,690 was the sample size and data collected through a questionnaire.

It was found that health professionals in general, had more positive attitude towards abortion than did students in teaching profession. The sex factor slightly obscured the relationships of the general differences of professions, but the strength of professional differences was sufficient to overcome the sex factor. A slight positive relationship was observed between class level in school and mean scale values of students responses on abortions.

Majority of the respondents were in favour of the school system as the educational channel for sex and family life education.

Bower and Christopher (1977) found that college students generally were approving of cohabitation as long as no children were involved and the couple was monogamous. Sixty percent of these students felt that cohabitation was appropriate in order to try out a relationship.

Orrawin (1977), studied the attitudes towards family planning and population education among 372 teachers and 687 adult students from four schools of each of four provinces of Thailand. Majority of them agreed that both family planning and birth control methods for adults should be advertised through the mass media.

Peplau Rubin and Hill (1977), studied 231 couples that has been called the Boston Dating Couples Study, they described three types of sexual attitudes into which the couples should be categorized. First, some of the couples were sexually traditional. This view is similar to precreational perspective in that premarital sex usually is seen as unacceptable. Such abstinence often is based on religious books. Some of the other couples were placed into the category of sexually moderate. These couples disapprove of casual sex but feel that premarital sex is acceptable if the partners are in love. This attitude is similar to the relational perspective. The largest group of couples in the Peplau et al. Study were labeled sexually liberal. This view is similar to a recreational orientation. For these respondents premarital sex is appropriate as long as both people agree, no emotional involvement is required.

Sompray (1981), studied Thai perspective teachers opinion towards family life and family planning including sex education. Main objectives of the study were to determine the opinions of prospective teachers towards family life and family planning including sex education. Sample consisted of 900 fourth year teacher trainees from 15 colleges of education throughout the country were drawn from two groups those who had studied sex education as a subject and others who had not. Questionnaire contained 100 items on a rating scale.

Major findings showed that both groups supported the family life and family planning courses that include sex education and concurrently backed up the offering of more courses in the colleges of education. The findings strongly supported the need for improving the curriculum and instruction regarding family life and family planning including sex education in the colleges of education.

Mata Ragnon (1982), studied 'Sex and the Filipino Adolescent: A Review'. It was found that Filipino adolescents were having more liberal attitudes towards sex growing openness towards sex related issues however did not mean that Filipino students were moving towards a new morality or permissiveness. Filipino adolescent were being caught in a period of transition. For example, on virginity it is generally valued it was no longer regarded in an absolute way as it was a generation ago. Female virginity was still more highly valued than male virginity, suggesting the endurance of double standards, 25 per cent adolescent accepted premarital sex.

The results of the study also showed that Filipino adolescent lacked knowledge of such technical medical aspects of ovulation, menstruation and fertilization, source of information regarding sex was best friends. They had open attitude towards family planning, masturbation and homosexuality and abortion. Adolescent crushes were very common. 50 per cent adolescents had gone for dating. Masturbation seemed more common in males.

The study also revealed that about 78 per cent of young men masturbate as compared to 5.4 per cent young women. Adolescents face problems like accidental pregnancy, inadequate sex education, girl–boy emotional problem, anxieties over kissing and petting, homosexual and lesbian relationships, and affairs with married men.

Raymendo (1984), Major data source for this study was 1982 Young Adult Fertility Survey (YAFS) in Phillipines. YAFS involved 5,402 married and unmarried female respondents aged 15-24 years As per recommendations of the Report, in as much as prevention of premarital sexual activities is not possible in the foreseeable future, short term task should be undertaken to reduce the harmful effects of youthful sexual activities. Reduction of harmful consequences as per the Report can be done by:

(a) increasing awareness and enlightenment in sexual matters,

(b) providing them with wider and more meaningful sex education in school and work,

(c) providing individual counselling at more opportune times,

(d) providing services which will not exclude providing contraceptives, if necessary, and

(e) campaigning to make adult members of the society more open and understanding of the plight of the adolescent.

Basnayake, Sriani (1986), have worked on the knowledge and attitude about reproductive health among youth in Sri Lanka; a study in selected urban & rural communities. Survey revealed that in spite of the high level of literacy and improved system of communication in Sri Lanka many of ancient myths practices and taboos pertaining to human sexuality are still adhered to in both rural and urban sectors by educated and less educated. An overwhelming majority disapproved of premarital sex but approved of practicing family planning within the context of marriage. Average preferred marriage age for girls is 23 years and for boys 26 years shows trends in delayed age for marriage

Bell, Ruth et al. (1987) in their book 'Changing Bodies, Changing Lives: A Book for Teens on Sex and Relationships" included information on various aspects of adolescent sexuality. Written specifically for teens. Teens from around the United States were surveyed in order to determine the book's contents, and they have shared their unique perspectives on sexuality. This is one of the best resources available for teens.

Boew-Gutman, Sonia, (1987) in their book 'Teen Pregnancy' discussed values involving sexuality, health issues for adolescent mothers and their babies, contraception, parenting readiness, the economics of raising a child. The book includes five case studies of pregnant teens, and offers advice for teens who think they may be pregnant.

Hendrick & Hendrick (1987a, 1987c, 1988) have done extensive research on the relationship between love attitudes and sexual attitudes. They noted, "The study of love and sexuality as companion variables is one of our goals in close relationship research, because it is apparent to us that trying to separate love from sexuality is like trying to separate fraternal twins: they are certainly not identical, but, nevertheless, they are strongly bonded". The Hendricks have developed scales to measure both sexual attitudes and love attitudes.

Hendrick & Hendrick (19876c) listed six love styles and an example item for each is given below:

- Eros (romantic, passionate love): "I feel that my lover and I are meant for each other."
- Ludus (game-playing love): "I enjoy playing the 'game of love' with a number of different partners."
- Storage (friendship love): "The best kind of love grows out of a long friendship."
- Pragma (logical, practical love): "It is best to love someone with a similar background."
- Mania (possessive, dependent love): "When my lover doesn't pay attention to me, I feel sick all over."
- Agape (selfless love): "I would rather suffer myself than let my lover suffer."

Hendrick and Hendrick (1987c) found that the more times an individual reported that he or she had been in love, the more permissive were his or her standards. Yet being in love currently was associated with less permissive standards. In their study, permissiveness also was related to different styles of love. More specifically, greater permissiveness was associated with ludus (gamelike love), and less permissiveness was associated with agape (selfless, giving love), storage (platonic or friendship love), and pragma (practical love).

Hendrick and Hendrick (1988) found that respondents who were in love were less permissive and less instrumental than respondents not in love. They stated, "Love and sexuality are strongly linked to each other and to both the physical and spiritual aspects of the human condition. For romantic personal relationships, sexual love and loving sexuality may well represent intimacy at its best".

Cobliner (1988), has found that true to convention, the majority of men might prefer but do not require emotional involvement to have sex, whereas the majority of women will not have sex without it. He discovered that college students are wary of each other: men are afraid of women's emotional needs and demands for time, whereas women fear abandonement, but both sexes are likely to become sexually involved without emotional commitment. Reasons for engaging in sex differ more by sex than sexual orientation, more similarities are found in lesbians and heterosexual women, and gay men and heterosexual men respectively.

Reiss (1989) developed a multiple item scale combining the separate questions on male and female into one by eliminating the gender reference (the items do not include she or he) and changing the affectional level to (a) without much affection, (b) moderate affection, (c) strong affection and (d) love relationship. For example, "I believe that premarital intercourse is acceptable if one is in a love relationship."

The other self-administered scales have been developed to measure sexual standards. The original Reiss scale has been criticized for using outdated terms (e.g., full sexual relations, not including some common forms of sexual behaviour (e.g. oral-genital sex), and using relational categories that are somewhat ambiguous and not mutually exclusive (e.g. in love, engaged).

Scott and Griffin (1989), found the main reasons for not using condoms, even when they were available, were "drunkenness, 'losing control and not caring', and being worried about partner's response to the idea." Reasons reflecting this age and stage of development. However, communication difficulties are not unique to heterosexual relationships.

Sabogal et al. (1991) listed the following reasons for having anal intercourse without a condom among the men in their sample of Latino gays and bisexuals aged 18 to 30 years in San Francisco, taken in the summer of 1990. In this sample of 100, men averaged 2.46 partners per month, 13.71 in the previous year.

The facts that militate against safer sex include those that relate to the evaluation of a potential partner, lack of communication about sex between partners, judgement, about the risk involved in a behavour or situation, lack of self control, the effects of alcohol, ambivalence about having sex, and the inability to consider alternatives to intercourse.

Chauliac Raimbault (1992) One important finding in his report is that the psychological and social consequences of adolescent pregnancy depend on the acceptance of family and of society. In many cultures the single pregnant adolescent carries the feelings of shame and guilt and hides her condition from her family and society for as long as possible due to fear of a lack of understanding and of rejection. A pregnant adolescence in many countries is forced to leave school. Urbanization, socio-economic pressure, and female education have a tendency to dispel this traditional attitude. Interventions to reduce adolescent pregnancy and its consequences include accessible contraceptives and access to good quality prenatal care.

Baldwin et al (1992) contended that students' reports of sexual behaviour in their study were accurate because they replicated earlier studies. They found Asians more sexually conservative than other groups, being significantly less likely than Blacks or Whites to have ever engaged in vaginal and oral sexual relations, and they began vaginal sexual relations about a half year lates than Whites. Latinos were significantly less likely to have ever engaged in vaginal and oral sexual relations but used condoms a greater percentage of the time for anal sex, effects that again disappeared when (unspecified) background variables were controlled for Asians used condoms for vaginal intercourse approximately 10% more of the time than Whites, and African Americans used condoms about 15% more. African Americans also used more effective means of birth control. They found that Latinos used contraception 11.5% less often than other ethnic groups, but the effect disappeared when (unspecified) "mediating" variables were controlled for. Although students had used birth control over 80% of the time, their level of usage left ample room for improvement – perhaps most surprising was the low level of use of spermicide and condoms that protect not only from pregnancy but also from STDs. Spermicide was essentially an ignored means of reducing STD transmission; even the CDC (1993) neither encouraged nor discouraged its use at the time of this study because it considered there were insufficient data to recommend it. Condoms were used an average of 31.1% of the time during vaginal intercourse in the prior 3 months of Baldwin et al.'s (1992) study, up from 23% in an earlier study. Women did have fewer partners than men; older students had fewer per year than younger students. Socioeconomic variables showed little effect on sexual behaviour, but they were slightly correlated with increased sexual liberalness and decreased sexual caution.

ICRW (1996) conducted multidisciplinary research in five areas of nutrition, acquired immuno-deficiency syndrome (AIDS), poverty and adolescent fertility and reproductive health in Caribbean and India.

One of the important findings related to sexuality is that cultural expectations that young women will be passive in sexual matters and the equation of condom use with infidelity and mistrust are placing them at risk of AIDS and other sexually transmitted diseases. The programmes that target adolescent fertility are available, as in the Caribbean, they will be underutilised if they do not serve the expressed needs of the target population and ensure confidentiality.

2.4 Conclusion

During the past several decades, attitudes towards sexual activity have changed dramatically. Views regarding premarital sex, extramarital sex and specific sexual acts are probably more open and permissive today than they have been at any time in recent history. Young people are exposed to sexual stimuli on television and in magazines and motion pictures to a greater extent than ever before. Effective methods of birth control have lessened the fear of pregnancy. All these changes have given adolescence more freedom. These changes also produce more conflict, however, since guidelines for "appropriate behaviour" are less clear-cut than they were in past. In some families, the divergence between adolescence and parental standards of sexual morality is great.

It is clear from the literature reviewed earlier that education about sex and sexuality has been a controversial issue since its evolution in India (Mehta, Saxena and Mukherjee, 1969). Even its reference in the school curriculum has been objected to, what to talk of Sex Education as 'Education' often naming it as 'Adolescence Education' and 'Self Awareness Education'.

It is also evident from the review of the literature that whatever researches have been undertaken, there do not cover all the components of sex education and also few studies only sampled either students or teachers for finding out their perceptions about sex and sexuality. Looking into the trends and filling the gap, the present study includes all the components of sex education namely its need, gender equality, homosexuality, virginity, peer-group dependence, monogamy, role of media, deviant behaviour, social approval, role of religion and morality, individual responsibility, undesirable life styple,dating, myths/misconceptions and heterosexuality have been covered and focusses on perceptions and values of the adolescents students and their teachers. The area of research undertaken is of great importance as has been considered by UNESCO which is of the view:

> *Human Sexuality in its moral dimensions needs special attention as it has dearth of research work in the area which is useful for the educationists, curriculum framers and most important for policy framers for future course of action. (UNESCO, 1994)*

3

Methodology and Procedure

3.1 Introduction

The present chapter deals with methodology consisting of the sample, design, variables, tools and statistical devices used in the study. After having gained insight from the literature related to the problem, the rationale and objectives of the present study, related methodology and empirical design for the research problem have been delineated. All these aspects have been discussed in this chapter.

A number of methods are available for conducting a research study.. Research studies adopting different methods do not as a rule, differ significantly in their procedure. Selection, formulation and definition of the problem review of related literature, sensing and defining a problem, formulating hypothesis, constructing tools, collection, analysis and interpretation of data are steps common to all types of methods of research.

The type of data collected for this research study and procedure followed to collect it, normally puts the study under survey type method. Surveys are concerned with condition or relationship that exists, practices that prevail, beliefs and view points or attitudes that are held, processes that are going on, effects that are being felt or trends that are developing. In short, they describe and interpret what exists at present.

The main objective of the present study is to study the values and perceptions of the adolescent students and teachers related to sex and sexuality.

3.2 Variables

3.2.1 Independent Variables

3.2.1.1 Adolescent Students

Age Adolescent students in the age group of 15-18 years studying at secondary or senior secondary level have been taken for the study.

Sex Both male and female students of these levels form another independent variable.

Socio-economic status (SES) of the students at low, middle and high level is another variable in determining the sex and sexuality related values and perceptions (SSRVPs) of the subjects.

3.2.1.2 Teachers, only those teachers who actually teach the above sampled students in the school at senior or senior secondary level have been taken for the study.

Sex, both male and female teachers form independent variable.

Grade, PGT and TGT grade teachers have been taken as independent variable

3.2.2 Dependent variable

Sex and Sexuality Related values and Perceptions (SSRVPs) of the subjects are influenced by independent variables i.e. SES level or being male or female. sex and sexuality related values and perceptions relating to students and teachers have been taken as dependent variable for the study.

3.2.3 Control of the Relevant Variables

The control of the relevant variables in the study other than independent variables is very essential, for these may also affect the dependent variables and make the results spurious. Therefore these variables must be kept constant, so that they may operate equally in all conditions of the study or they be removed from all conditions of the study and their effects on dependent variables may be balanced or cancelled. The following variables were thought to be relevant and were controlled in the study:

(i) **Students' Educational level:**
Adolescent students only studying in secondary or senior secondary classes have been considered. This controls their educational level.

(ii) **Age**
Adolescent students of age group 15-18 years were taken for the study.

(iii) **Teachers**
Only those teachers are included in the study who have taught the students taken in the sample.

(iv) **Socio-Cultural Background**
Adolescent students studying in Kendriya Vidyalayas of South Delhi were taken thereby providing the same socio-cultural setting.

3.3 Design & Conditions of the Study

The study is related to sex and sexuality related values and perceptions of adolescent students and their teacher. Design of the study covering students and teachers is given below:

3.3.1 Adolescent Students

The study of sex and sexuality related values and perceptions of adolescent students both boys and girls and three levels of their socio-economic status has been done. Male and female adolescent students of class X, XI and XII falling in the age group of 15-18 years were taken as representative of students. The study forms 2X3 factorial design as shown in the diagrammatically in Fig 3.1.

Fig. 3.1

SES-wise Distribution of Adolescence Students

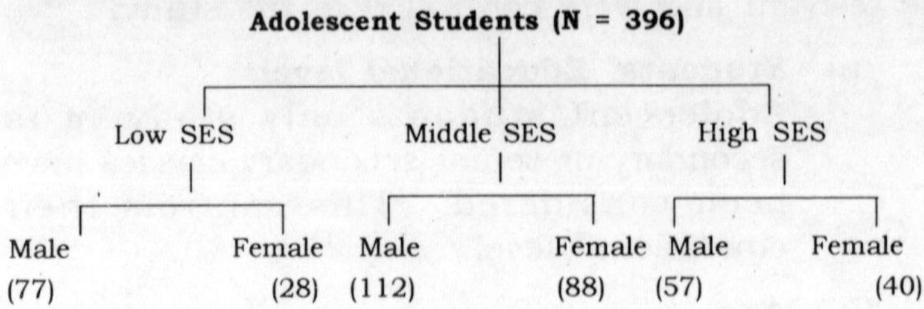

In Part I of the study, adolescent students have been considered gender wise and on socio-economic status (SES) at low, middle and high levels. This followed a 2X3 factorial design consisting of following groups:

1. First group of students consisted of 77 males of low SES
2. Second group of students consisted of 112 males of middle SES
3. Third group of students consisted of 57 males of high SES.

4. Fourth group of students consisted of 28 females of low SES.
5. Fifth group of students consisted of 88 females of middle SES.
6. Sixth group of students consisted of 40 females of high SES.

The combination of these groups has been shown diagrammatically below:

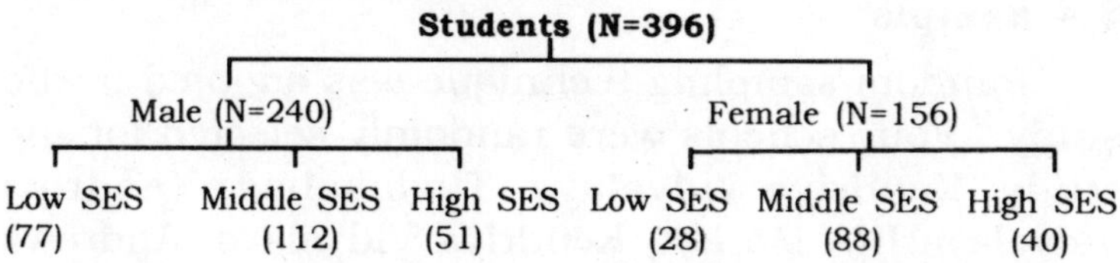

Fig. 3.2. SES-wise Distribution of Male and Female Students

3.3.2 Teachers

Sex and Sexuality Related Values and Perceptions (SSRVPs) of male and female teachers of TGT and PGT grades have been included in a 2X2 factorial design as given below:

(1) The first group consisted of 15 male TGTs from four Kendriya Vidyalayas from South Delhi

(2) The second group consisted of 15 male PGTs from four Kendriya Vidyalayas.

(3) The third group consisted of 68 female TGTs from same schools.

(4) The fourth group consisted of 46 female PGTs of the same schools.

The combination of four groups of subjects employed in the study are diagrametically shown in the following table:

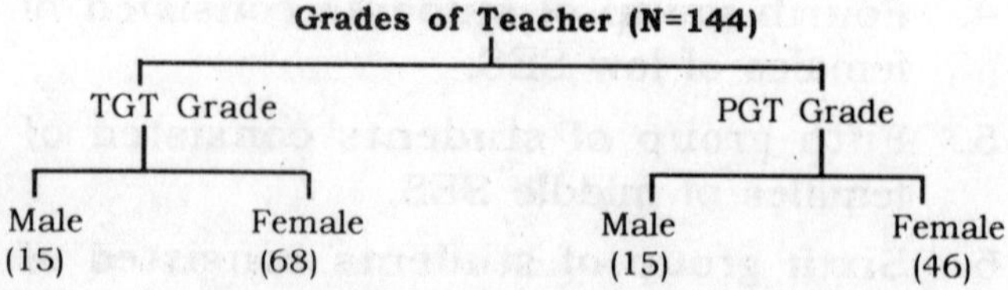

Fig. 3.3. Sex and Grade-wise Distribution of Teachers

3.4 Sample

Random sampling technique was adopted in the study. Four schools were randomly selected for the study: Kendriya Vidyalaya, Tuglakabad; Kendriya Vidyalaya INA Market; Kendriya Vidyalaya, Andrews Ganj and Kendriya Vidyalaya, Sadiq Nagar. The number of students and teachers taken from the four Kendriya Vidyalayas has been given in the Table 3.1.

Table 3.1

Sample of Students and Teachers from Various Kendriya Vidyalayas

Kendriya Vidyalayas	No. of Students	No. of Teachers
Tuglakabad	70	22
INA Market	76	34
Andrewsganj	180	66
Sadiq Nagar	70	22
Total	396	144

The schools selected for the present study were situated in the same district of South Delhi. Convenience of the researcher to operate in the vicinity of her residence and also Jamia being situated in South Delhi, are two reasons to select schools in South Delhi randomly.

The Teachers who have taught/are teaching the sampled students have been taken as the sample of teachers.

144 teachers and 396 students from the four Kendriya Vidyalaya were selected as a sample of the study. Grade-wise total number of teachers and sex-wise number of students have been given in table 3.2.

Table 3.2

Total Number of Adolescent Students and Teachers

	Teachers			Students		
School	**TGT**	**PGT**	**Total**	**Boys**	**Girls**	**Total**
Four	83	61	144	240	156	396

Sex and grade–wise sample of a total of 144 teachers is shown below in table 3.3.

Table 3.3

Sex and Grade-wise Distribution of Teachers

Teachers Status	Male	Female	Total
TGT	15	68	83
PGT	15	46	61
Total	30	114	144

Gender and status-wise sample of students out of a total of 396 students is being given in table below:

Table 3.4

Gender and Status wise Distribution of Students

Socio-economic Status (SES)	Male	Female	Total
Low	77	28	105
Middle	112	88	200
High	51	40	91
Total	240	156	396

3.5 Hypotheses

The following hypotheses are formulated on the basis of the objectives delineated in the Chapter 1 and tested empirically:

1. There is no significant difference in sex and sexuality related values and perceptions of adolescent students and their teachers.
2. There is no significant difference in sex and sexuality related values and perceptions of male and female adolescent students.
3. There is no significant difference in sex and sexuality related values and perceptions of adolescent students belonging to low, middle and high SES.
4. There is no significant difference in sex and sexuality related values and perceptions of male and female students of low SES.
5. There is no significant difference in sex and sexuality related values and perceptions of male and female students of middle SES.
6. There is no significant difference in sex and sexuality related values and perceptions of male and female students of high SES.

7. There is no significant difference in sex and sexuality related values and perceptions among male students of low, middle and high SES levels.
8. There is no significant difference in sex and sexuality related values and perceptions among female students of low, middle and high SES.
9. There is no significant interactional effect of Sex and SES on sex and sexuality related values and perceptions of students.
10. There is no significant difference in sex and sexuality related values and perceptions of TGT and PGT teachers.
11. There is no significant difference in sex and sexuality related values and perceptions of males of TGT and PGT grade.
12. There is no significant difference in sex and sexuality related values and perceptions of females of TGT and PGT grades.
13. There is no significant difference in sex and sexuality related values and perceptions of males and females TGT grade.
14. There is no significant difference on in sex and sexuality related values and perceptions of male and female PGT grade teachers.
15. There is no significant difference in sex and sexuality related values and perceptions of male and female teachers.
16. There is no significant interactional effect of sex and being TGT or PGT on sex and

sexuality related values and perceptions of teachers.

3.6 Tools of Data Collection

Selection and development of tool constitutes an important part of a research study. As per the requirement of the design, the following tools are adopted/developed for collecting the data as per the objectives of the study:

3.6.1 Socio-Economic Status (SES) Scale

SES scale developed by Hasnain and Srivastava (1999) was used to determine SES of the students.

The scale comprised of 45 items pertaining to various socio-economic levels that determine the status with varying weightages to items/sub-items in the form of scores. Educational level, Professional level, membership in various social organisation, accommodation and its type, household gadgets, other facilities and social interactions available are the major dimensions covered to ascertain SES levels.

Validity and Reliability of SES Tool

SES Scale used in the study had concurrent validity with Kulshrestha's tool (1986) as .736. Reliability of the tool was .998 based on test retest method.

The scores achieved by the students on socio-economic status scale were tabulated. Students represented in Q_4 were put in high socio-economic status. Students in Q_2 and Q_3 were put in middle SES level. Students in Q_1 were taken as low SES level. 105 students obtained scores 63.5 and below were taken as low SES representing Q_1. 200 students obtained scores between 64 and 93.5 were taken to be of middle SES. Students obtaining 94 and above were taken as High SES group, they were 91 in number. They were kept in low and high SES levels respectively the students obtaining scores between Q_1 and Q_3 were treated as middle SES group. Fig. 3.4 shows the number of students falling in various categories of SES.

Fig. 3.4

Diagrammatic presentations of Conditions or Groups of Part I

Students (N=396)

- Low SES
  - Male (N=77)
  - Female (N=28)
- Middle SES
  - Male (N=112)
  - Female (N=88)
- High SES
  - Male (N=51)
  - Female (N=40)

It is clear from the table that :

105 students falling in low SES group included 77 male students and 28 female students.

200 students representing middle SES group included 112 males cases and 88 female cases.

91 students representing high SES group were 51 male cases and 40 female cases.

Thus a total of 396 students on three SES levels were taken for the present study.

3.6.2 Scale of Sex Related Values and Perceptions Scale

Tools are the educational instruments through which the desired objectives are tested. To measure the sex and sexuality related values and perceptions of the sampled students and teachers, a tool was to be constructed. So construction of the SRVPs scale was undertaken. Before preparing the tool, a thorough study was done. The literature on sex education and its curricula developed by

UNESCO (1972) Education Department, Hongkong, UNESCO (1991), NCERT (1992), SECRT (1993), Watsa (1994), was consulted.

3.6.2.1 Procedure of Tool Construction

106 Items were framed based on knowledge, attitude trends, etc. reported in related literature. As study was to be conducted on the adolescent students and their teachers, the test items were discussed with 10 teachers and 50 students. This was to ascertain the face validity of items from the point of view of content and language of the items. 36 items were excluded based on the discussion with teachers and students. Thus only 70 items were retained.

Scale of 70 items were discussed with the teacher educators, experts in Population Education and Sex Education. Their opinion on various aspects of the items of the tool, its nature, relevance, language and area covered was sought and 14 items were dropped. Scale having 56 items was used for data collection from the sample teachers and students of pre-test.

3.6.2.2 Validity of Sex and Sexuality Related Values and Perceptions Scale

As stated by Garret and Woodword (1966, P. 354) "Establishing the validity of a test is of utmost importance. The validity of a test or any measuring instrument, depends upon the fidelity with which it measures what it purports to measure."

According to Gronlund and Linn (1990), "Validity refers to the extent to which the evaluation result serve the particular uses for which they are intended. It interprets the results rather to the instrument and its presence is a matter of degree that is always specific to some particular use".

Validity is a relative term. A test is valid for a particular purpose or in a particular situation - it is not generally valid.

3.6.2.2.1 Content Validity by Means of Judgement

Content validity refers to which a test measures a representative sample of the domain of tasks under consideration. it is especially in values and perception testing and is determined by making a logical analysis of test contents and comparing to the domain of values and perceptions to be scaled. The validation of content through competent judgement is most satisfactory when the sampling of items is wide and judicious and when adequate standardization groups are utilized.

Less defensible than content validity is the judgement process called "face validity". A test is said to have face validity when it appears to measure whatever the investigator had in mind, namely what she thought she was measuring.

Judgement of face validity is very useful in helping an investigator to decide whether her test items are relevant to some specific situations or to specialized occupational experiences.

As regarding the validity of sex and sexuality related values and perceptions scale, the investigator showed it to the Population Education experts and Pedagogues. The experts examined and analyzed the content of each test item in relation to the instructional objectives, the pedagogue maxims, etc. They also gave their opinion regarding the correctness and completeness of the test items developed for sex and sexuality related values and perceptions scale. Their suggestions were taken into account to improve the test items. Hence, the content validity of the tool for sex and sexuality related values and perceptions was established.

Following suggestions relating to various items were taken into consideration while giving opinion about the scale.

(i) Statement may not be a fact;

(ii) Negative statements may countercheck the responses;

(iii) Statement are to be made in easy language and terminology; and

(iv) Statement should cover one theme only.

Based on the above suggestions 14 items were rejected by the experts, 56 items were retained.

A scale having 56 items was printed and pretested on 50 students and 15 teachers as per the details given below in tables 3.5 and 3.6.

Table 3.5

Sample of the Students for the Pre-test

	Students (N=50)		
Class	**Male**	**Female**	**Total**
X	12	10	22
XI	13	15	28
Total	25	25	50

Table 3.6

Sample of Teachers for the Pre-test

	Teachers (N=15)		
Sex	**TGT**	**PGT**	
Male	3	2	5
Female	4	6	10
Total	7	8	15

3.6.2.3 Result of Item Analysis

Responses of students and teachers were on three point scale of agree, undecided and disagree in the weightage of 3, 2 and 1 respectively. On this basis they were scored and total score was obtained for each subject on the sex and sexuality related values and perceptions scales of the tool administered having 56 items. The items having difficulty level between 25-75% and discriminating value between 20-80 have been accepted. Eleven items were deleted and 45 items were accepted on this basis. Thus the final form of the tool has been prepared.

3.6.2.4 Concurrent Validity of Sex and Sexuality Related Values and Perceptions Scale

In the third place the concurrent validity of the test was calculated by comparing the scores of students (N=50) on the attitude scale standardized by Hasnain (1986) and on the present tool. the co-efficient of correlation came out to be 0.64 which is significant at 0.05 level. So the scale was thought to be valid tool for measuring sex and sexuality related values and perceptions of teachers and students.

3.6.2.5 Reliability of Sex and Sexuality Related Values and Perceptions Scale

Reliability refers to the consistency of a test results, how consistent or error free the measurements are. It is the consistency of scores obtained by the same individuals on different occasions or with different sets of individuals on different occasions.

There are four procedure in common use for computing the reliability co-efficient of a test. These are:

1. Test-retest (repetition)
2. Alternate or parallel forms
3. Split half technique
4. Rational equivalence

All of these methods furnish estimates of the reproducibility of test scores; some times one method and sometimes another will provide better measure. Reliability of sex and sexuality related values and perceptions scale has been established as follows:

Fig. 3.5

Reliability of SSRVPs Scale

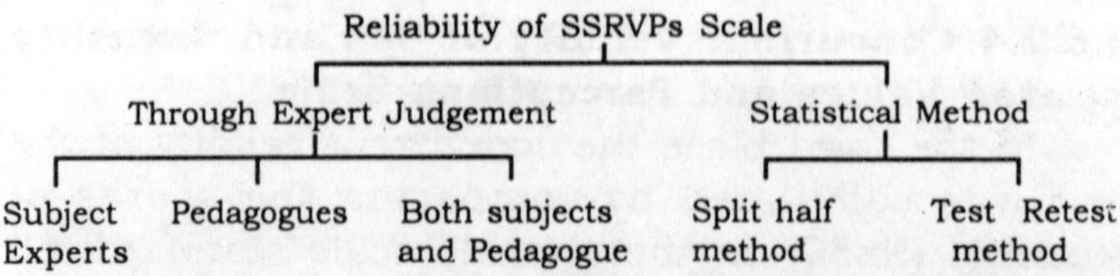

(a) Reliability through Expert Judgement. This was established by showing sex and sexuality related values and perceptions scale to subject experts and pedagogues.

(b) Statistical Method. Reliability of the sex and sexuality related values and perceptions was established statistically also.

Split Half Method

Investigator used split half method to establish the reliability of the tool. The test was split into two reasonably equivalent halves by taking even and odd items separately. These independent halves are then used as a source of the two independent scores needed for reliability estimation Correlation coefficient of odd and even is 0.41 which is significant at 0.01 level. This values indicates it to be fairly high positive correlation between two halves. Since, number of respondents was 540. Therefore, 45 items in the scale are reliable. Spearman-brown formula is used to obtain the full length test reliability.

Test and Re-test Method

Sampled students were administered the SSRVPs test and scores were obtained. The test was again administered on the same students after a gap of 15 days. The scores so obtained were correlated with the previous scores. The coefficient of correlation was found to be 0.86. This indicated a high correlation coefficient thus establishing the test to be reliable one by this method.

3.6.2.6 Final Sex and Sexuality Related Values and Perceptions Scale

The 45 items of sex and sexuality related values and perceptions, which could be standardized as per procedure described above, were given to population and sex education experts and pedagogues. 15 broad components were identified by the experts into which the 45 items have been put.

Components of Sex and Sexuality Education and Their Related Values and Perceptions

The 45 items on the scale were discussed with three experts to categorise them into major components relating to sex and sexuality education. The experts categorise the items into 15 components. The main components and the related values and perceptions which are labelled as V_1 to V_{15} are given below:

V_1	**Need for Sex Education**
Sl. No.	**Related Values and Perceptions in the Scale**
1	All the students should be given information about sex and sexual behaviour
10	Teenagers should discuss their sex problems with their friends
17	Special Counselling cells should be setup in schools to provide information on sex
18	Sex education is as important as any other education for the teenagers
19	Parents should not feel shy of giving correct information to children about sex
29	Sex education in schools can create unnecessary curiosity among children about sex
33	To save children from becoming victims of sex crimes, it is important to impart sex education to them
38	Sex problems need not be discussed with the parents/ teachers
34	family life and sex education should be taught to young and old to control population of our country

V_2	**Gender Equality**
Sl. No.	**Related Values and Perceptions in the Scale**
5	A student may have a good friend of opposite sex with no sexual purposes
32	Young people should freely interact with the opposite sex
2	Mother and father should be equally responsible for the birth and care of child.

V_3	**Homo Sexuality**
Sl. No.	**Related Values and Perceptions in the Scale**
45	Homosexuality is abnormal sex/social behaviour

V_4	**Virginity**
Sl. No.	**Related Values and Perceptions in the Scale**
9	Virginity is a gift to be given to life partner
22	Unwed mothers should not be discarded by the society
41	Having pre-martial sex is socially and morally wrong

V_5	**Peer Group Dependence**
Sl. No.	**Related Values and Perceptions in the Scale**
10	Teenagers should discuss their sex problems with their friends

V_6	**Monogamy**
Sl. No.	**Related Values and Perceptions in the Scale**
11	One should have only one sex partner in life

V_7	**Role of Media**
Sl. No.	**Related Values and Perceptions in the Scale**
12	TV and films excite sexual desires in boys and girls
35	Explicit sex in movies is the biggest threat to Indian culture

V_8	**Deviant Behaviour**
Sl. No.	**Related Values and Perceptions in the Scale**
4	Frustration among out of non-fulfilment of sex desires, has added to students' socially undesirable behaviour of youth
13	Constant sexual frustration leads students to violent social behaviour

V_9	**Social Approval**
Sl. No.	**Related Values and Perceptions in the Scale**
15	Parents must given freedom to teenagers to make friends of either sex
36	Wearing a perfectly descent top with a skirt/jeans by the girls should not be objectionable
37	Inviting a girl/boy friend to one's house should be discouraged by family members
39	One should go for an arranged marriage as parents are better judges of people than the youngsters

V_{10}	**Role of Religion and Morality**
Sl. No.	**Related Values and Perceptions in the Scale**
8	Feeling of guilt and desire to be faithful towards one's future life partner keeps one away from premarital sex
20	Controlling sex desires shows a person's good moral character
24	Marriages are held only for gratification of sex desire
25	Other qualities of life partner are of no value if he/she becomes sexually unfit
42	Staying of unmarried people is immoral
31	Sex should be practiced with one's married life partner only

V_{11}	**Sex Crime**
Sl. No.	**Related Values and Perceptions in the Scale**
23	One should help in the rehabilitation of victim of sexual crime
21	Girls should not take lift in the vehicles belonging to strangers

V_{12}	**Lifestyle**
Sl. No.	**Related Values and Perceptions in the Scale**
7	It is undesirable to go to pubs, discos and late night parties
26	Dance party generally has sexual intentions

V_{13}	**Dating**
Sl. No.	**Related Values and Perceptions in the Scale**
27	Meeting of boys and girls outside school/home is not meant only to establish sexual relations
28	Dating has become status symbol and adds to prestige
30	Teenagers should have choice of dating even if parents object to it
40	Dating is desirable as it is a means of interaction between the sexes
43	Dating is a means of interaction between the sexes but does not necessarily lead to sexual involvement

V_{14}	**Myths and Misconceptions**
Sl. No.	**Related Values and Perceptions in the Scale**
14	AIDS patients are social criminals and they must be kept out of society
44	Masturbation is a bad habit and can harm health

V_{15}	**Heterosexuality**
Sl. No.	**Related Values and Perceptions in the Scale**
3	Students do mischievous behaviour mainly to impress the opposite sex
6	Females dress-up beautifully mainly to impress males
Sl. No.	**Negative Statements of Related Values and Perceptions in the Scale**
14	AIDS patients are social criminals and they must be kept out of society
24	Marriages are held only for gratification of sex desires
25	Other qualities of life partner are of no value if he/she becomes sexually unfit
26	Dance party generally has sexual intentions
29	Sex education in schools can create unnecessary curiosity among children about sex
30	Teenagers should have choice of dating even if parents object to it
37	Inviting a girl/boy friend to one's house should be discouraged by family members
38	Sex problems need not be discussed with the parents/ teachers
44	Masturbation is a bad habit and can harm health

3.7 Procedure

Permission was obtained from Commissioner, Kendriya Vidyalaya Sangathan for conducting the study in four Kendriya Vidyalaya viz. : Kendriya Vidyalaya, Tuglakabad, Kendriya Vidyalaya INA Market, Kendriya Vidyalaya, Andrews Ganj and Kendriya Vidyalaya, Sadiq Nagar. Separate letters were issued to the heads of schools with necessary instructions.

The investigator visited the schools and data were collected within a fixed span of time for comparison between SRVPs of students and teachers.

The tool was administered simultaneously to the teachers and students of a school after giving them the preliminary instructions related to the tool.

3.8 Data Processing and Its Treatment

Research data become meaningful when they are analyzed and interpreted properly. Data collected was tabulated for sex and sexuality related values and perceptions of male and female adolescent students and teachers of the four schools.

Responses were taken on a three-point scale having different scores such as agree, undecided and disagree with the scores 3, 2 and 1, respectively. Negative items were reversed for scoring. After combining the score, total score of a student and a teacher were computed. After combining the scores of individual, group/sub-group–wise mean scores were calculated for further statistical analysis. 't' test was used to find out the significance of difference between mean scores of groups of students (gender-wise or SES level) and for groups of teachers (gender-wise as well as PGT/TGT grade wise). Duncan's Range test was applied to know inter-group differences both in case of students and teachers. ANOVA was applied to know the interactional effect of independent variables on dependent variables of the study.

The data analysis and its interpretation have been discussed in Chapter-4.

4

Analysis of Data – Findings and Discussion

4.1 Introduction

The requisite information pertaining to Sex and Sexuality Related Values and Perceptions (SSRVPs) is collected from two types of respondents, namely 144 teachers and 396 students with the help of a structured questionnaire designed for this study. The results so obtained from the data are being deliberated in three parts. Firstly, the Part I includes comparison of adolescent students and teachers on sex and sexuality related values and perceptions. Thereafter, the results obtained from the information by student respondents are discussed in Part II, followed by analysis of teacher respondents observations in Part III. So the present chapter has been divided into three sections.

Part I includes a comparative study of adolescent students and teachers on various sex and sexuality related values and perceptions; and their group means, standard deviations and t-test values have been derived. The results so obtained have been discussed in this part.

Part II deals with results obtained from the information given by adolescent students. Design for Part II entails 2X3 factorial design. In this part mean sex and sexuality related values and perceptions scores of students, standard deviations and t-test results have been given. For inter group comparison Duncan's Range Test has been used and ANOVA has been applied for the interactional effect of Sex and SES. Results obtained have also been analysed and interpreted.

Part III This part includes the results obtained from the teachers. 2X2 factorial design has been devised for teachers-sex and grade-wise. The scores have been presented in the form of mean sex and sexuality related values and perceptions scores, standard deviations, t-test. For inter-group comparison Duncan's Range Test has been applied and to study the interactional effect of sex and grades ANOVA has been used. Results so obtained have also been discussed and interpreted.

4.2 Components of Sex and Sexuality Education

The mean sex and sexuality related values and perceptions scores of each group are calculated on the basis of individual scores obtained by the subjects of various groups. Mean sex and sexuality related values and perceptions scores have been given in following tables for students and teachers. t-test or Duncan's Range Test is applied to see the significance of difference between various groups of students and teachers. t-value has been tested separately for knowing significance of difference between the groups on fifteen components of sex and sexuality related values and perceptions from Need for Sex Education (V_1) to Heterosexuality (V_{15}). ANOVA has been used to find out the interactional effect of independent variables of sex and SES/grades on fifteen components of sex and sexuality related values and perceptions separately for students and teachers. Fifteen components of sex and sexuality related values and perceptions have been discussed in detail in Chapter 3. Here, they are denoted as variable V_1 to V_{15} in all the tables related to different conditions of students and teachers as next page:

V_1 Need for Sex Education

V_2 Gender Equality

V_3 Homosexuality

V_4 Virginity

V_5 Peer Group Dependence

V_6 Monogamy

V_7 Role of Media

V_8 Deviant Behaviour

V_9 Social Approval

V_{10} Role of Religion and Morality

V_{11} Sex Crime

V_{12} Lifestyle

V_{13} Dating

V_{14} Myths and Misconceptions

V_{15} Heterosexuality

In following parts of the Chapter, sex and sexuality related values and perceptions has been denoted as SSRVPs.

Part I

4.3 Comparison on Sex and Sexuality Related Values and Perceptions between Adolescent Students and their Teachers

396 students and 144 teachers had given their responses on 45 items in the questionnaire developed by the researcher which have been clubbed in 15 components as denoted by V_1 to V_{15} in following table.

Mean, standard deviation and t-values for the students and teachers have been given in the following table 4.1.

Table 4.1

Mean SSRVPs Scores, Standard Deviation and results of t-test between Students and Teachers

Components/ variables	Students (N= 396)		Teachers (N= 144)		t-value
	Mean	SD	Mean	SD	
V_1	22.10	02.98	23.00	02.87	03.14**
V_2	08.02	01.00	08.01	01.22	00.15
V_3	02.77	00.54	02.87	00.40	01.95*
V_4	07.13	01.46	07.81	01.25	04.05**
V_5	02.42	00.82	02.45	00.85	00.37
V_6	02.78	00.58	02.88	00.46	01.82
V_7	05.12	01.15	05.62	00.89	04.76**
V_8	04.26	01.18	03.83	01.56	03.37**
V_9	09.43	01.69	09.53	01.77	00.60
V_{10}	14.99	02.07	15.89	02.03	04.47**
V_{11}	05.12	01.02	05.64	00.77	05.55**
V_{12}	04.75	01.12	05.08	01.10	03.10**
V_{13}	10.89	01.86	11.20	01.95	01.70

V_{14}	04.03	01.02	03.74	00.86	03.02**
V_{15}	03.82	01.42	03.44	01.33	02.78**

* Significant at .05 level

** Significant at .01 level

SSRVPs of students and teachers have been compared first by taking out their group means and SDs on components V_1-$V_{15.}$ t-test is applied and tested for significance. For components V_1, V_3, V_4, V_7, V_8, V_{10}, V_{11}, V_{12}, V_{14} and V_{15}, there is a significant difference between adolescent students and their teachers at either 0.05 level or 0.01 level. As per table 4.1, it is evident that on V_2, V_5, V_6, V_9, V_{13}, no significance difference is found between adolescent students and their teachers. Results have been discussed given next page:

For component 1 'Need for Sex Education' includes following value statements:

Sl. No.	Related Values and Perceptions in the Scale
1	All the students should be given information about sex and sexual behaviour
10	Teenagers should discuss their sex problems with their friends
17	Special Counseling cells should be setup in schools to provide information on sex
18	Sex education is as important as any other education for the teenagers
19	Parents should not feel shy of giving correct information to children about sex
29	Sex education in schools can create unnecessary curiosity among children about sex.

33	To save children from becoming victims of sex crimes, it is important to impart sex education to them
38	Sex problems need not be discussed with the parents/teachers
34	family life and sex education should be taught to young and old to control population of our country

Mean and SD values for Need for Sex Education for students are 22.10 and 2.98 and for teachers these values are 23.00 and 2.87. t-value came out to be 3.14 which is found to be significant at .01 level. Higher mean value of teachers show that they feel the need of sex education more than the students. Range of scores could be from 9 to 27. The mean values shows that both adolescent students and their teachers have positive attitude towards the need of introduction of sex education in schools. Myrdal (1968) considered the need for sex education to be logical and relevant when given along with family life education. Bhatwadekar and Israel (1970) also lay an emphasis on building positive attitude towards sex and family life. Balasubramaniam (1970) also consider the need for sex education as important in their study. Ministry of Education, Manila (1973), Nagda (1973), Alocious (1974) and Lee (1975) also support the same view. Sex Education is again favoured by Maitra (1994). In his findings it is considered as a measure to control birth.

George (1994) considers the inclusion of Sex Education as a measure to help prevention of AIDS. He regards this as an issue of sexual morality. SECRT (1992) and TOI (1998) reported sex education is a favoured idea by the Indian youth which again is in line with the findings of the present study. However some researchers reported that teachers were against the inclusion of sex education in schools. Ministry of Education (1973) held the view that school teachers do not favour sex education in school for the fear of promiscuity. Verma (1990) considers sex education as not so favourable subject since it may add the psychological, social and academic problems. Similarly Murthy (1991), Sharma (2000) and TOI (2000) show the trends of parents, teachers and students going against sex education in schools. Findings of Verghese (1970) also show that male and female teachers differed in their attitude towards population education and related matters. While IMRB survey (1997) has reported that younger people favoured sex education in schools more than older generations.

For component V_2 'Gender Equality' has been computed with the following statements:

No. 5	A student may have a good friend of opposite sex with no sexual purposes
No. 32	Young people should freely interact with the opposite sex
No.2	Mother and father should be equally responsible for the birth and care of child

For component V_2 Gender Equality, perusal of the table 4.1 shows mean and SD for students as 8.02 and 1.00 and for teachers it is 8.01 and 1.22. t-value comes out to be 0.15 which is not significant at .01 level or .05 level. So it shows that teachers and students agree on the value of Gender Equality equally thus accepting the Hypothesis I for this component. The Hypothesis I stated *"There is no significant difference on sex and sexuality related values and perceptions between students and teachers"*. Finding of present study are in agreement with SECRT (1992) and TOI (1998) where they support the value of Gender Equality.

However, Ryan and Cooper (1998) are of the view that Gender roles are taught at home and outside and hence there are differences in perception about Gender Equality.

For component V_3 'Homosexuality' value statement No.45 has been given:

Sl. No. in the Scale	**Related Values and Perceptions**
45	Homosexuality is abnormal sex/social behaviour

For component V_3 Homosexuality, perusal of the same table shows mean and SD for students as 2.77 and 0.54 and for teachers it is 2.87 and 0.40. t-value comes out to be 1.95 which is significant at 0.05 level which shows that teachers favour more strongly than their students. Burt (1985) has considered homosexuality as intimacy. The finding is in agreement with TOI (1998) survey where the survey found that Indian youth is uncomfortable with the concept of homosexuality. Findings are in consonance with Nag (1994) who considers it to be a risky behaviour and chances of contracting AIDS increase with it. Recently there are certain reports which show a legal coverage for homosexuality relationships in the western world. However, California Supreme Court (1969) considers professional competence more important than their homosexual behaviour. Ryan and Cooper (1996), Alamedia (2001) conveyed in their findings that students feel homophobic from such people.

The Component V_4 'Virginity' covers following value statements:

Sl. No. in the Scale	Related Values and Perceptions
9	Virginity is a gift to be given to life partner
22	Unwed mothers should not be discarded by the society
41	Having pre-martial sex is socially and morally wrong

On this component, mean and SD values are 7.13 and 1.46 for students and 7.81 and 1.25 for teachers and the t-value is 4.05. This is found to be significant at .01 level. Higher mean in case of teachers means they favour virginity more than their students. Virginity has been favoured overwhelmingly by respondents in Sri Lanka (Basnayake, 1986). Lower mean value in case of students (7.13) however shows the effect of permissiveness about sexual matters.

The value covered in the component V_5 'Peer Group Dependence' is:

Sl. No. in the Scale	Related Values and Perceptions
10	Teenagers should discuss their sex problems with their friends

For component V_5 Peer Group Dependence, perusal of the same table shows mean and SD for students as 2.42 and 0.82 and for teachers it is 2.45 and 0.85. t-value comes out to be 0.37 which is not significant at .05 level or .01 level. Thus accepting the hypothesis I for the value component of Peer Group Dependence.

However, the study by Patel (1974), Murthy (1981), and TOI (2000) found that sex education should be imparted so that students do not fall on peer group for various misleading information and conceptions.

The value statement for the component (V_6) 'Monogamy' is:

Sl. No. in the Scale	**Related Values and Perceptions**
11	One should have only one sex partner in life

For component V_6 Monogamy, perusal of the same table shows mean and SD for students as 2.78 and 0.58 and for teachers it is given to be 2.88 and 0.46. t-value comes out to be 1.82 which is not significant at .05 level or .01 level. Thus accepting the hypothesis I for the value component of Monogamy. This conveys the agreement of students and teachers for value of Monogamy. Such opinion was also endorsed by the survey report of Marg (1994) and Kala (1995) where Monogamy has been hailed against premarital sex.

For component V_7 'Role of Media' following value statements have been given:

Sl. No. in the Scale	Related Values and Perceptions
12	TV and films excite sexual desires in boys and girls
35	Explicit sex in movies is the biggest threat to Indian culture

On perusal of the same table 4.1 on component V_7, Role of Media mean and SD value are 5.12 and 1.15 for students and 5.62 and 0.89 for teachers. it gives a t-value of 4.76 which is significant at .01 level. Higher mean in case of teachers signifies that they agree more strongly on the view that media does influence Sex and sexuality related values and perceptions of students. They see it as a threat to the Indian culture.

Gupta (1974), Gaugrade (1975), Chhabra (1992) and Kapoor (1996) hold the views that knowledge sources of literature and movies do impress upon adolescent's sex and sexuality related values and perceptions. However, SECRT (1992) and Kumar (2001) consider that media has acquired a role of third parent and is adding to development of dangerous attitude among adolescents which may lead to lowering the order of society.

The component V_8 'Deviant Behaviour' has been computed with following statements:

Sl. No. in the Scale	**Related Values and Perceptions**
4	Frustration among out of non-fulfilment of sex desires, has added to students' socially undesirable behaviour of youth
13	Constant sexual frustration leads students to violent social behaviour

The mean and SD values as calculated are 4.26 and 1.18 for students and 3.83 and 1.56 in case of teachers. t-value comes out to be 3.37 which is significant at .01 level. Higher mean value in case of students meant they agree more with the views that frustrated students show more deviant behaviour while teachers see deviant behaviour not so much related to sex and sexuality. Madaras (1986) opined that deviant behaviour could emerge due to too much pressures, expectations and feelings of being unloved. So, she suggested for better communication skills by teachers and parents.

Deviant behaviour has its roots in sex and sexuality related values and perceptions of students has been the view of Crow and Crow (1965). Upmanya and Sushma (1994) visualise it in their studies that adolescent depression is a serious problem in India and it may have its relation to sex role orientation. SECRT (1992) however reported in their findings that process of change from orthodox to liberal sexual behaviour has been slow despite the onslaught of media and modernising influences.

The Component V_9 'Social Approval' has been covered in the following statements:

Sl. No. in the Scale	Related Values and Perceptions
15	Parents must given freedom to teenagers to make friends of either sex
36	Wearing a perfectly descent top with a skirt/ jeans by the girls should not be objectionable
37	Inviting a girl/boy friend to one's house should be discouraged by family members
39	One should go for an arranged marriage as parents are better judges of people than the youngsters

For component V_9 Social Approval, perusal of the same table shows mean and SD for students as 9.43 and 1.69 and for teachers it is given to be 9.73 and 1.77. t-value comes out to be 0.62 which is not significant at .05 level or 0.01 level. Thus accepting the hypothesis I for the value component of Social Approval. Sangwan (2001) however opines that teenagers do not care for social approval under peer pressure for fashion and friends of opposite sex.

For component V_{10} 'Religion and morality', the following value statements are included:

Sl. No. in the Scale	Related Values and Perceptions
8	Feeling of guilt and desire to be faithful towards one's future life partner keeps one away from premarital sex

20	Controlling sex desires shows a person's good moral character
24	Marriages are held only for gratification of sex desires
25	Other qualities of life partner are of no value if he/she becomes sexually unfit
42	Staying together of unmarried people is immoral
31	Sex should be practiced with one's married life partner only

Role of Religion and Morality, calculated mean and SD values for students are 14.99 and 2.07 and for teachers, these are 15.89 and 2.03 respectively, and calculated t-value is 4.47 which is found to be significant at .01 level. Higher value of me an in case of teachers show that religion and morality control Sex and sexuality related values and perceptions is more than perceived by the students. Brown (1981) has also opined in his work that religious setting influences Sex and sexuality related values and perceptions positively.

For V_{10} SECRT (1992) and Chhabra (1992) support the findings of present study. Moral values conveyed through value education and sex education do influence sex and sexuality related values and perceptions of students and teachers positively, and they are in a better position to take wiser decisions.

Being raised in a religion is predicted to lead to more conservative sexual behaviour and less cautious contraceptive and STD-related behaviour because of the inability of a religious adolescent to acknowledge sexual activity (Baldwin, Whiteley, and Baldwin, 1992; Fine, 1988); however, Baldwin et al.

Found no effect of religious background on sexual activity. White and DeBlassie (1992) noted a substantial inverse correlation between adolescent sexual behaviour and religious participation. Accordingly to their study, those with an allegiance to the church are more likely to heed its sanctions against sexual activity and to feel more guilt when they don't. Wyatt and Lyons-Rowe (1990, p.519-522) found that father's educational level, childhood religiousness, and adult religiousness were insignificant with respect to African American women's sexual satisfaction, although childhood church attendance was negatively related. Although these studies suggest mixed and sometimes contradictory effects of religion on sexual behaviour and sexual satisfaction, the effect of religious upbringing on sexual communication or negotiation remain uninvestigated.

These findings are not supported however by Nag (1994) and Kathulia (1999) who report more liberal attitude of women relating to faithfulness to life partner. Nagpal 2001 reports that students are not able to hold their desires. He opined further that lust is being confused with love and adolescents are not able to understand the difference so they behave liberally.

For V_{11} component 'Sex Crime' has been covered under the values statements:

Sl. No. in the Scale	Related Values and Perceptions
23	One should help in the rehabilitation of victim of sexual crime
21	Girls should not take lift in the vehicles belonging to strangers

For Sex Crime, the calculated mean and SD values are 5.12 and 1.02 for students, and 5.64 and 0.77 for teachers – t-value is 5.55 which is significant at 0.01. level. The results show that two groups differed on Sex Crime Higher mean in case of teachers show that they favour more precautionary behaviour and a sympathetic attitude for victims as compared to their students.

For V_{12} Component 'Life Style' is covered under the following value statements:

Sl. No. in the Scale	Related Values and Perceptions
7	It is undesirable to go to pubs, discos and late night parties
26	Dance party generally has sexual intentions

Life Style calculated mean and SD values are 4.75 and 1.12 and 5.08 1.10 for students and teachers respectively. t-value comes out to be 3.10 which is found to differ significantly at .01 level on Life Style The mean value shows that teachers perceive going to pubs, discos or parties as more undesirable than their students. On the other hand, students also find it less agreeable that dance party has sexual intentions. Times of India (1999) has similar reports whereby teenagers want more freedom to stay late night out and go to pubs and discos which may make some parents to worry about their well being.

For V_{13} 'Dating' has been covered under the following value statements:

Sl. No. in the Scale	Related Values and Perceptions
27	Meeting of boys and girls outside school/ home is not meant only to establish sexual relations
28	Dating has become status symbol and adds to prestige
30	Teenagers should have choice of dating even if parents object to it
40	Dating is desirable as it is a means of interaction between the sexes
43	Dating is a means of interaction between the sexes but does not necessarily lead to sexual involvement

For component V_{13} Dating, perusal of the same table shows mean and SD for students as 10.89 and 1.86 and for teachers it is given to be 11.20 and 1.95. t-value comes out to be 1.70 which is not significant at 0.05 level or 0.01 level. Thus accepting the hypothesis I for the value component of Dating. The findings are in conformity with the opinion of Rahul (1977) but Mata Ragnon (1982) and TOI (1998) differ in opinion saying that middle class parents have conservative attitude on the issue of Dating Behaviour.

The component V_{14} 'Myths and Misconceptions' covers the value statements:

Sl. No. in the Scale	Related Values and Perceptions
14	AIDS patients are social criminals and they must be kept out of society
44	Masturbation is a bad habit and can harm health

For Myths and Misconceptions, mean and SD values are 4.03 and 1.02 for students 3.74 and 0.86 for teachers. t-value is 3.02 which shows that two groups differed significantly at .01 level on this component Lower mean in case of students signifies that they are less informed than their teachers and also that the teachers hold a sympathetic attitude towards AIDS patients. Basnayake (1986) has reported similar findings where the survey revealed that in spite of the high level of literacy and improved system of communication in Sri Lanka, many of ancient myths, practices and taboos pertaining to human sexuality are adhered. Such confusions lead to guilt and anxiety in later part of life. In present study higher mean in case of teachers show that they are correctly informed against myths while lower mean in case of students show their adherence to older values leading to many myths such as masturbation is harmful to health.

These findings have been supported by studies undertaken by George (1994), Weilands (1997), Chugh (1990) and Survey of TOI (2000) where they point out existence of myths and misconceptions in society on the issue of masturbation and hence support sex education for the removal of misleading ideas on sex and sexuality related values and perceptions of young and old.

The component V_{15} 'Heterosexuality' covers the values statements as given below:

Sl. No. in the Scale	Related Values and Perceptions
3	Students do mischievous behaviour mainly to impress the opposite sex
6	Females dress-up beautifully mainly to impress males

For Heterosexuality (V_{15}) perusal of table 4.1 shows mean and SD values as 3.82 and 1.42 in case of students, and 3.44 and 1.33 in case of teachers. t-value is 2.78 which shows that two groups differed significantly on Heterosexuality at 0.01 level.

These findings of Murthy (1991) and Watsa (1992) show that old and young Indian generation favour heterosexuality more than homosexuality. Although, there are historical evidences that homosexuality existed in Indian society since ages.

On the basis of the above analyses, it can be concluded that:

For components of sex and sexuality education and values and perceptions covered under the components V_2, V_5, V_6, V_9 and V_{13}. retained hypothesis 1 i.e. *"There is no significant difference between sex and sexuality related values and perceptions of adolescent students and their teachers".*

For components of sex and sexuality education: V_1, V_3, V_4, V_7, V_8, V_{10}, V_{11}, V_{12}, V_{14}, and V_{15} and values and perceptions covered under these components. Hypothesis No.1 is rejected.

Part II

Part II comprises of Sex and Sexuality Related Values and Perceptions (SSRVPs) of students and comparison of the groups sex-wise and at various levels of SES (Low, Middle and High SES levels). Table 4.2 to 4.9 present mean, SD and t-value for students.

Table 4.2
Mean SSRVPs Scores, Standard Deviation and results of t-test between the means of Male and Female Adolescent Students

	Male (N= 240)		Females (N= 156)		t-value
variable	Mean	SD	Mean	SD	
V_1	22.62	02.94	21.30	02.87	04.39**
V_2	08.12	01.00	07.87	00.99	02.43*
V_3	02.74	00.57	02.82	00.46	01.43
V_4	07.10	01.49	07.19	01.42	00.64
V_5	02.41	00.83	02.46	00.81	00.28
V_6	02.75	00.62	02.81	00.52	01.01
V_7	05.17	01.13	05.03	01.17	01.18
V_8	04.26	01.25	04.25	01.6	00.10
V_9	09.26	01.73	09.71	01.60	02.59**
V_{10}	14.89	02.22	15.15	01.88	01.20
V_{11}	05.16	01.05	05.08	00.99	01.CO
V_{12}	04.67	01.19	04.89	01.01	02.06*
V_{13}	11.06	01.93	10.65	01.76	02.03*
V_{14}	04.08	01.03	03.99	01.01	00.61
V_{15}	04.11	01.38	03.39	01.37	05.11**

*Significant at .05 level.
**Significant at .01 level.

4.4 Comparison of SSRVPs of Male and Female Adolescent Students

240 male students and 156 female students had given their responses on 45 items in the questionnaire which have been clubbed in 15 components as they have been described in Chapter 3.

In table 4.2 sex-wise mean and standard deviations have been given for V_1 to V_{15}. To compare the two groups t-test is applied and tested for its significance of difference. For V_1 – Need for Sex Education Mean and SD value for male students are 22.62 and 2.94. Mean and SD value for female students are 21.30 and 2.87. t-value is found to be 4.37 which is significant at 0.01 level. This shows that male and female students differed significantly on the component of 'need for sex education'. Higher mean score for male students on 'Need for Sex Education' shows that they agree more favourably for it as compared to its female counterparts. The findings are in line with Khan (2001) where boys favour sex education more than girls and with LLewallyn (1986) where the author agreed that sex and sexuality related difference in boys and girls have socio-cultural basis. However, Patel (1974) found that girls are more knowledgeable than boys on the matters of sex and reproduction.

Padilla and O'Grady (1987, found Mexican American University of California students in Southern California significantly more conservative than Angle students on measures of autoeroticism, heterosexual relations, and abortion. Women were more conservative than men concerning abortion, and both were more likely to endorse sexual myths and have less sexual knowledge. They found Mexican Americans less sexually experienced, more likely to use condoms, and less likely to use oral contraceptives than European Americans. Mexican American men were more sexually experienced than women (in contrast to Chinese American students), including more likely to have engaged in same-sex behaviour.

For Gender Equality, mean value and SD value are 8.12 and 1.00 for male students while 7.87 and 0.99 for female students and t-ratio is 2.43 which is significant at .05 level. Higher mean value in case of male students show that they perceive Gender equality more favourably than the female students. While as per the general observations in society and in the opinion of Ryan and Cooper (1996) that boys enjoy more attention than girls at school and home. Although boys enjoy more social favour but they have favoured Gender Equality more than the female students.

Many researchers have found, that, true to convention, the majority of men might prefer but do not require emotional involvement to have sex, whereas the majority of women will not have sex without it (e.g., Carroll, Volk, & Hyde, 1985; Earle & Perricone, 1986; Gilligan, 1982; Leigh, 1989). Cobliner (1988) discovered that college students are wary of each other: men are afraid of women's emotional needs and demands for time, whereas women fear abandonment, but both sexes are likely to become sexually involved without emotional commitment. Reasons for engaging in sex differ more by sex than sexual orientation, according to Leigh, who found more similarities between lesbians and heterosexual women, and gay men and heterosexual sexual men, respectively.

There is another possibility for explaining reasons for having sex, beyond stereotypical gender role behaviour. The conception of the relationship between emotions and sexual desire may be articulated differently by sex. Emotions may be antecedent, component, or consequence of sexual behaviour or some combination of the three.

Scott and Griffin (1989), found the main reasons for not using condoms, even when they were available, were "drunkenness, 'losing control and not caring', and being worried about partner's response to the idea." Reasons reflecting this age and stage of development. However, communication difficulties are not unique to heterosexual relationships.

Sabogal et al. (1991) listed the following reasons for having anal intercourse without a condom among the men in their sample of Latino gays and bisexuals aged 18 to 30 years in San Francisco, taken in the summer of 1990. In this sample of 100, men averaged 2.46 partners per month, 13.71 in the previous year.

The facts that militate against safer sex include those that relate to the evaluation of a potential partner, lack of communication about sex between partners, judgement, about the risk involved in a behavour or situation, lack of self control, the effects of alcohol, ambivalence about having sex, and the inability to consider alternatives to intercourse.

On 'Social Approval' component, mean and SD values are 9.26 and 1.73 for male students and 9.71 and 1.60 for female students, t-value is found to be 2.59 which is significant at .01 level. This shows that male and female respondents differed significantly on 'Social Approval' component. Higher value of mean is in favour of female students and it shows that females consider social permission more important than that of male students. This finding has been in line with Watsa (1992) where social permission is not considered as so important by male youth as compared to the female youth. This may also be due to female's self-perception of their roles. Similarly Basnayake (1986) had found in his study that youth disapproved of premarital sex in Sri Lanka.

Singh (1980) analyzed data from a national probability sample of adults for 5 years between 1972 and 1978. Singh reported a gradual decrease over time in the percentage of respondent who said that premarital sex is always wrong.

Studies by Mahoney (1978); Ferrell, Tolone, and Walsh (1977); King, Balswick, and Robinson (1977); and Robinson and Jedlicka (1982) all found evidence for a decrease in the traditional double standard and an increase in more permissive premarital standards for men and women during the 1970s. Yet not all of the recent research completely supports this conclusion, Lawrance, Robinson, and O'Rourke (1984) reported support for stable, rather than increasingly permissive, premarital sexual attitudes across three times periods – 1972, 1977, and 1982.

Research on sexual standards from the late 1970s/ early 1980s through the late 1980s is also not entirely consistent. Most researchers argue that this era is characterized by a continued liberalization of sexual standards, with the standards of permissiveness either with or without affection more prevalent, and the traditional double standard less prevalent (e.g., Darling et al., 1984; Robinson & Jedlicka, 1982; Walsh, 1989). In a comparison of sexual standards for dating relationships of college students at one Midwestern college in 1982 and 1988; Bishop and Lipsitz (1991) found that both men and women students in the 1988 sample were significantly more liberal in attitudes about premarital intercourse than were the students in the 1982 sample. Robinson, Ziss, Ganza, and Katz (1991) described data collected from college students over a period of 20 years (1965 to 1985). From the students' responses to a 5-item premarital attitude scale, the researchers concluded that a consistent decrease in negative attitudes about premarital intercourse occurred. When looking at promiscuity (how immoral or sinful it is to have many partners), however, they found that a large percentage of male and female respondents in the 1980s than in the 1970s viewed promiscuity negatively. Across the years of the study, the attitudes toward promiscuity in females were more negative than the attitudes toward promiscuity in males (a double standard).

Many possible reasons have been proposed for the probable trend away from more conservative standards toward greater permissiveness. In particular this trend is related to other changes in society since World War II, such as technological innovations that decrease the risk of pregnancy and/ or simplify birth control (e.g. the pill) increasing political liberalism, the women's movement, and the influence of sexual messages in the mass media

(King et al., 1977; Walsh, 1989). We argue that some of what appears to be inconsistent results (a recent trend toward more conservative standards) actually reflects a new transition period in sexual standards for dating relationships; that is, in the early to mid-1980s; AIDS began to receive mass media attention. Due to time lags in attitudinal change and in research studies of such change, we have only begun to see hints of this trend in the last few years – the late 1980s to early 1990s.

Hendrick and Hendrick (1987c) found that the more times an individual reported that he or she had been in love, the more permissive were his or her standards. Yet being in love currently was associated with less permissive standards. In their study, permissiveness also was related to different styles of love. More specifically, greater permissiveness was associated with ludus (gamelike love), and less permissiveness was associated with agape (selfless, giving love), storage (platonic or friendship love), and pragma (practical love).

Hendrick and Hendrick (1988) found that respondents who were in love were less permissive and less instrumental than respondents not in love. They stated, "Love and sexuality are strongly linked to each other and to both the physical and spiritual aspects of the human condition. For romantic personal relationships, sexual love and loving sexuality may well represent intimacy at its best".

Component 'Life Style' has mean and SD values as 4.67 and 1.19 for the male students while 4.89 and 1.01 for female students. t-value is out as 2.06 which is found to be significant at .05 level. Higher mean value for female students indicated they held Life Style view more strongly than male students which suggested that female students consider going to pubs and discos and dance parties undesirable. Findings of Marg – India Today survey (1994) has been similar to findings of present study. Survey also shows that metro cities have youth who have accepted western life style and behaviour.

For Heterosexuality related values and perceptions mean values and SD values are 4.11 and 1.38 for male students and 3.39 and 1.37 for female students. t-value is 5.11 which shows that difference is significant at .01 level. Higher mean value for males indicated that they favoured this view more strongly than the female students. This means male students agree more than female students and do different behaviour relating to sexuality to impress the other sex.

Other components of Sex and sexuality related values and perceptions such as Homosexuality, Virginity, Peer Group Dependence, Monogamy, Role of Media, Deviant Behaviour, Role of Religion and Morality Myths and Misconceptions are found to be insignificantly different hence retaining the hypothesis No.2 for these variables which states *"There is no significant difference in sex and sexuality related values and perceptions of male and female adolescent students".*

4.5 Comparison of SSRVPs of Students of Different Socio Economic Status

To determine the SES level of student respondents, the scores on Hasnain & Srivastava (1999) Scale are tabulated. Scores falling on Q_1 and below, they present low SES, scores falling in Q_2 and Q_3 represent middle SES group and scores falling above Q_3 represent high SES group of students. This has been discussed in detail in

Chapter 3. Mean and SD values on Sex and sexuality related values and perceptions have been given in table 4.3 for the three SES level of the students separately for V_1 to V_{15}.

Table 4.3

Mean Scores of Low, Middle and High Socio-Economic Status groups of Adolescent Students on SSRVPs and result of Duncan's Range Test

Value	Low SES (A) Mean (N=105)	Middle SES (B) Mean (N-200)	High SES (C) Mean (N=91)	A VS. B	A VS. C	B VS. C
V_1	22.15	22.07	22.10	-	-	-
V_2	07.90	07.96	08.30	-	*	*
V_3	02.67	02.80	02.85	*	*	-
V_4	06.90	07.13	07.42	-	*	-
V_5	02.45	02.40	02.44	-	-	-
V_6	02.79	02.77	02.79	-	-	-
V_7	05.00	05.15	05.20	-	-	-
V_8	04.31	04.30	04.10	-	-	-
V_9	09.10	09.38	10.00	-	*	*
V_{10}	14.83	14.96	15.26	-	-	-
V_{11}	05.10	05.13	05.13	-	-	-
V_{12}	04.79	04.79	04.62	-	-	-
V_{13}	10.80	10.84	11.10	-	-	-
V_{14}	04.26	03.93	04.00	*	-	-
V_{15}	03.85	03.78	03.90	-	-	-

* Significant at 0.05 level

\- Not significant

In order to make comparison between the mean Sex and sexuality related values and perceptions scores of three groups of students, i.e., low, middle and high SES levels, Duncan's Range Test (McGuigan, 1969) is applied. The results of various comparisons have been explained below:

Perusal of the table 4.3 reveals that mean Sex and sexuality related values and perceptions score on component Gender equality (V_2) are 7.90, 7.96 and 8.30. The difference between high SES group of adolescent students and low SES group and also between middle SES group and high SES group are significant at 0.05 level, showing these groups differed on the gender equality value at significant level. Higher mean value 8.30 for High SES group shows a higher agreement for gender equality.

Mean value for the component, 'Homosexuality' for three groups namely low, middle and high SES grades are 2.67, 2.80 and 2.85. The difference between two groups of low vs middle and low vs high is found to be significant at .05 level.

On the variable 'Virginity' mean values for low, middle and high SES groups comes out to be 6.90, 7.13 and 7.42 respectively. Difference between high vs low SES group is significant at 0.05 level while other groups show no significant difference at this variable. This clearly shows that students of High SES favour 'Virginity' more for themselves than low SES students. Kothari (2001) however opined that Indian male irrespective of their educational level favour for virgins as wives.

Following the same table, mean value for Sex and sexuality related values and perceptions relating to V_9 'Social Approval' for the three SES groups i.e. low, middle and high is 9.10, 9.38 and 10.93 respectively. Bhattacharya and Joshi (1995) found in their study that Girls of low educational level have early marital and premarital sexual relation. This could be due to social and cultural norms restricting sexual behaviour. Difference between low and high SES group, as well as middle vs high High SES group is found to be significant at 0.05 level. This clearly meant that SES students seek and favour social permission for making friends and wearing cloths of their choice. They also value permission for inviting friends of opposite sex.

On Myths and Misconceptions, mean values of 4.26, 3.93 and 4.00 comes out for low, middle and high SES groups of students. Difference between low and middle group is found to be significant at .05 level.

Mean value of 4.26 is highest for low SES group for 'Myths and Misconceptions' which shows that they agreed more with these than middle and high SES groups. Lower class has more of myths and misconceptions which could be due to many factors related to SES. International Planned Parenthood Federation (1985) has emphasised that most far reaching influence on pattern of sexual life has been that of economic change and social change that has invariably followed in its wake. Economic status influenced the sexuality.

Baldwin et al. (1992) noted that studies on U.S. college compuses find that socioeconomic and ethnic variables are not important predictors of sexual behaviour. They expected age to affect sexual and contraceptive behaviour, older students would be more circumspect in their sexual behavour, use more reliable means of contraception, and use contaception more frequently than younger people. Women would be more conservative in their sexual behaviour and more careful in their contraceptive practices than men. Being raised mainly by both original parents was predicted to result in increased conservative sexual behavour.

Comparison of the three groups is found to be insignificantly different on values and perceptions of the components Peer Group Dependence, Monogamy, Role of Media, Deviant Behaviour, Role of Religion and Morality, Sex Crime, Life Style, Dating and Heterosexuality. Thus for these components hypothesis No.3 which states that *"There is no significant difference in Sex and sexuality related values and perceptions of adolescent students belonging to low, middle and high SES levels" is retained.*

4.6 Comparison of Sex and Sexuality Related Values and Perceptions of Male and Female Students of Low SES Group

The hypothesis No.4 states that "**There is no significant difference between male and female students of low SES group**". In order to compare Sex and sexuality related values and perceptions of the male and female students of low SES, t-test is applied to look for any significant difference between two genders of students belonging to low SES. There are 77 males and 28 female students of low SES. t-test is applied for V_1 to V_{15} components separately. The findings have been given in Table 4.4.

Table 4.4

Mean Scores of Low Socio-Economic Status group of Students on SSRVPs and result of t-test between their means

	Male (N= 77)		Females (N= 28)		t-value
Value	**Mean**	**SD**	**Mean**	**SD**	
V_1	22.69	02.68	20.68	03.02	03.28**
V_2	08.01	00.98	07.61	00.92	01.91

V_3	02.58	00.71	02.89	00.32	02.21*
V_4	06.81	01.57	07.14	01.41	01.00
V_5	02.48	00.79	02.36	00.83	00.70
V_6	02.82	00.53	02.71	00.66	00.83
V_7	05.04	01.21	04.86	01.24	00.68
V_8	04.35	01.29	04.21	01.10	00.50
V_9	08.99	01.68	09.43	01.79	01.17
V_{10}	14.68	01.94	15.25	01.79	01.37
V_{11}	05.07	01.07	05.18	00.98	00.49
V_{12}	04.68	01.07	05.11	00.92	01.90
V_{13}	11.00	01.81	10.25	01.53	01.95*
V_{14}	04.31	01.00	04.11	00.99	00.93
V_{15}	04.05	01.35	03.29	01.41	02.55*

* Significant at 0.05 level.

** Significant at 0.01 level.

Table 4.4 depicts that the mean, SD and t-values for Sex and sexuality related values and perceptions of components V_1 to V_{15}. Mean for male and female students of V_1 are 22.69 and 20.68. SDs for them comes out as 2.68 and 3.02. t-value is 3.28 which shows that two sex differed significantly on the value 'Need for Sex Education' at 0.01 level. Higher mean for male students suggested their favourable perception for Need for Sex Education.

For value Homosexuality mean values are 2.58 and 2.89 for male and female students respectively. SD values are 0.71 and 0.32 for them respectively. t-value of 2.21 shows the difference between two groups to be significant at .05 level on the variable 'Homosexuality'. The findings show that the female students of Low SES consider it more objectionable than male students. Khan (2001) has reported in his study that 3% of adolescents have homosexual sex.

On perusal of the same table, for value component 'Dating' mean values for two sexes are 11.00 and 10.25 respectively with SDs being 1.81 and 1.53 for male and female students. t-value 1.95 comes out to be significant at .05 level.

In a study comparing attitudes about extramarital and extradating sexual relationships, Margolin (1989) found that female subjects felt that sexual infidelity was equally unacceptable in both types of relationships, whereas male subjects felt that sexual infidelity in a dating relationship was less unacceptable than in a marriage relationship.

Mean values for Heterosexuality, are 4.05 and 3.29 & SD values are 1.35 and 1.41 respectively for male and female students. t-value is 2.55 which happens to be significant at 0.01 level. It shows that two sexes differ significantly on the component 'Heterosexuality'. Males of low SES agree to the statements No. 3 and 6 relating to the component which means that they behave in certain ways to impress the opposite sex.

On other variables: Gender Equality, Virginity, Peer Group Dependence, Monogamy, Role of Media, Deviant Behaviour, Social Approval, Role of Religion and Morality, Sex Crime, Life Style and Myths and Misconceptions t-values are found to be insignificant proving the hypothesis 4 to be true for them which states *"There is no significant difference in sex and sexuality related values and perceptions of male and female students of low SES level"*.

4.7 Comparison of Sex and Sexuality Related Values and Perceptions of Male and Female Students of Middle SES Group

Hypothesis 5 states that *"There is no significant difference in sex and sexuality related values and perceptions of male and female students of middle SES level"*. Middle SES is represented by 200 students in all. 112 male and 88 female respondents represented the two genders. Mean, SD and t-test is applied to see if there is any significant difference between the groups. Findings are given in Table 4.5.

Table 4.5

Mean Scores of Middle Socio-Economic Status group of Students on SSRVPs and result of t-test run among their means

	Male (N= 112)		Females (N= 88)		t-value
Value	Mean	SD	Mean	SD	
V_1	22.57	03.14	21.43	02.86	02.65**
V_2	08.03	01.03	07.88	01.00	01.05
V_3	02.83	00.48	02.75	00.53	01.12
V_4	07.13	01.47	07.13	01.48	00.04
V_5	02.38	00.85	02.43	00.83	00.47
V_6	02.73	00.64	02.81	00.52	00.88
V_7	05.25	01.06	05.01	01.19	01.49
V_8	04.21	01.26	04.41	01.06	01.16
V_9	09.19	01.81	09.61	01.63	01.69
V_{10}	14.95	02.27	14.97	01.92	00.06
V_{11}	05.19	01.05	05.05	00.92	01.00
V_{12}	04.73	01.16	04.85	01.08	00.75
V_{13}	11.03	01.92	10.60	01.73	01.62
V_{14}	03.91	00.96	03.95	01.06	00.31
V_{15}	04.06	01.42	03.41	01.34	03.30**

**Significant at 0.01 level

For the components of 'Need for Sex Education' mean value is 22.57 for male and 21.43 for females. SD values are 3.14 and 2.86 for male and female respectively. t-value comes out to be 2.65 which is significant at 0.01 level. It shows that two groups differed on Need for Sex Education significantly. Higher value of mean 22.57 is for male students which shows that they favoured Need for Sex Education more than their female counterparts. This finding is an agreement with that of Low SES students where the results have been the same.

On the value component of 'Heterosexuality' following statements were included in the tool. On perusal of the same table 4.5, 'Heterosexuality' component shows means of 4.06 for males and 3.41 for females. SD values are 1.42 and 1.34 for male and female students. T-value is 3.3 is significant at 0.01 level. It shows that two sexes differed significantly on Heterosexuality. This finding is again same in case of Low and Middle SES group males and females students.

On all other variables Gender Equality, Homosexuality, Virginity, Peer Group Dependence, Role of Media, Deviant Behaviour, Social Approval, Role of Religion and Morality, Sex Crime, Life Style, Dating, Myths and Misconceptions, the two sexes showed difference to be insignificant. Hence, most part of the hypothesis No. 5 is accepted which states that *"There is no significant difference in SSRVPs of male and female students of middle SES level"*.

4.8 Comparison of Sex and Sexuality Related Values and Perceptions of Male and Female Students of High SES Group

Hypothesis 6 states that there is no significant difference in sex and sexuality related values and perceptions of male and female students of high SES level". High SES is represented by 57 male and 40 female students. So in all 97 respondents represented high SES group as detailed in chapter III. Mean, SD and t-test are applied to see if there is any significant difference between two genders. Findings have been given in Table 4.6.

Table 4.6

Mean Scores of High Socio-Economic Status Group of Students on SSRVPs and Result of t-test between their Means

	Male (N= 57)		Females (N= 40)		t-value
Value	Mean	SD	Mean	SD	
V_1	22.60	02.91	21.45	02.80	01.91
V_2	08.49	00.90	08.05	00.99	02.22*
V_3	02.78	00.50	02.93	00.35	01.51
V_4	07.45	01.35	07.38	01.31	00.27
V_5	02.39	00.85	02.50	00.78	00.62
V_6	02.71	00.67	02.90	00.38	01.63
V_7	05.19	01.17	05.20	01.04	00.02
V_8	04.24	01.18	03.93	00.91	01.33
V_9	09.80	01.52	10.10	01.34	00.97
V_{10}	15.09	02.34	15.47	01.85	00.83
V_{11}	05.24	01.01	05.00	01.13	01.04
V_{12}	04.45	01.36	04.83	00.93	01.49
V_{13}	11.14	02.08	11.05	01.93	00.20
V_{14}	04.00	01.18	04.00	00.91	00
V_{15}	04.29	01.38	03.40	01.43	03.03**

* Significant at 0.05 level.

** Significant at 0.01 level

To compare the male and female students of high SES group t-test is applied.

For Gender Equality (V_2), mean scores for two sexes are 8.49 and 8.05 respectively and SD values are 0.90 and 0.99. t-value is 2.22 which is significant at 0.05 level. This implies that two sexes differ significantly on the variable Gender Equality. Higher means in case of male students show that they favour Gender Equality more than the female respondents. On the value of Gender Equality only males of High SES group differed significantly from rest of the categories of respondents. This could be attributed to socio-cultural milieu and their low self-perception.

On Heterosexuality two sexes show mean values to be 4.29 and 3.40 respectively. 1.38 and 1.43 are the SD for male and female students. t-value of 3.03 shows the difference to be significantly high at 0.01 level.

On all other values Need for Sex Education, Homosexuality, Virginity, Peer Group Dependence, Monogamy, Role of Media, Deviant Behaviour, Social Approval, Role of Religion and Morality, Sex Crime, Life Style, Dating and Myths and Misconceptions, the difference is found to be insignificant for two sexes.

4.9 Comparison of Male Students of Low, Middle and High SES Levels

In order to make inter group comparison of males at different SES levels, Duncan's Range Test is applied. 77 respondents represented low, 112 represented middle and 57 respondents are high SES male students as described in the Chapter III. Low SES group has been denoted as 'A', Middle SES group as 'B' and High SES group respondents as 'C'.

Table 4.7

Mean SSRVPs Scores and Results of Duncan's Mean Range Test among Male Students of Low, Middle and High SES Levels

Value	Means (Male Students)			Group Comparison		
	Low (A) N=77	Middle (B) N-112	High (C) N=57	A/C	A/C	A/C
V_1	22.69	22.57	22.61	-	-	-
V_2	08.01	08.03	08.49	-	*	*
V_3	02.58	02.83	02.78	*	-	-
V_4	06.81	07.13	07.45	-	*	-
V_5	02.48	02.38	02.39	-	-	-
V_6	02.82	02.73	02.71	-	-	-
V_7	05.04	05.25	05.20	-	-	-
V_8	04.35	04.21	04.24	-	-	-
V_9	09.00	09.20	09.80	-	*	*
V_{10}	14.68	14.95	15.10	-	-	-
V_{11}	05.06	05.19	05.24	-	-	-
V_{12}	04.68	04.73	04.45	-	-	-
V_{13}	11.00	11.02	11.14	-	-	-
V_{14}	04.31	03.91	04.00	*	-	-
V_{15}	04.05	04.06	04.29	-	-	-

* Significant at 0.05 level
\- Not significant.

To find out inter group differences on SSRVPs among male students of different SES, Duncan's range test is applied. For value Gender Equality (V_2), three groups of low, middle and high SES show means as 8.01, 8.03, 8.49 respectively. Difference is found to be significant at 0.05 level – for males of Low SES and High SES, also for Middle SES and High SES males. Higher mean value in case of High

SES respondents show that they value gender equality more than their middle and low SES counterparts. This could be due to their different socio-cultural values.

For Homosexuality (V_3), mean values for three groups are 2.58, 2.83 and 2.78 respectively. Low SES male and middle SES male have the difference to be significantly high at 0.05 level

For variable component 'Social Approval', mean values are 9.00 and 9.24 and 9.80 respectively for 3 SES strata of male. Difference is significantly high at 0.05 level for following group comparisons i.e. Low vs High SES male and Middle vs High SES male. The SSRVPs component of Myths and Misconceptions has been covered under the following value statements:

For 'Myths and Misconceptions' mean values for three groups are 4.31, 3.91 and 4.00 respectively. Difference is found to be significantly high at 0.05 level between high and middle SES male subjects. Higher means of Low SES male students show that they agree more with component Myths and Misconceptions. For 'Need for Sex Education', Peer Group Dependence, Monogamy, Role of Media, Deviant Behaviour, Role of Religion and Morality, Sex Crime, Life Style, Dating, Heterosexuality, the differences are found to be insignificant. Thus it retained the hypothesis No.7 which states that *"There is no significant difference in sex and sexuality related values and perceptions among male students of low, middle and high SES levels"*.

4.10. Comparison of Sex and Sexuality Related Values and Perceptions of Female Students of Low, Middle and High SES Groups

In order to make inter group comparison of females at different SES levels, Duncan range test is applied. 28 respondents represented low, 88 represented middle and 40 respondents are high SES female students as described in Chapter III.

Table 4.8

Mean SSRVPs Scores and Results of Duncan's Mean Range Test among Female Students of Low, Middle and High SES Levels

Value	Means (Female Students) Low (A) N=28	Middle (B) N-88	High (C) N=40	A/B	A/C	B/C
V_1	20.68	21.43	21.45	-	-	-
V_2	07.61	07.88	08.05	-	-	-
V_3	02.89	02.75	02.93	-	-	-
V_4	07.14	07.13	07.38	-	-	-
V_5	02.36	02.43	02.50	-	-	-
V_6	02.71	02.81	02.90	-	-	-
V_7	04.86	05.01	05.20	-	-	-
V_8	04.21	04.41	03.93	-	-	*
V_9	09.43	09.61	10.10	-	-	-
V_{10}	15.25	14.97	15.48	-	-	-
V_{11}	05.18	05.05	05.00	-	-	-
V_{12}	05.11	04.85	04.83	-	-	-
V_{13}	10.25	10.60	11.05	-	-	-
V_{14}	04.11	04.95	04.00	-	-	-
V_{15}	03.29	03.41	03.40	-	-	-

* Significant at 0.05 level.

To find out intergroup comparisons of female students belonging to different SES, Duncan's Mean range test is applied as shown in table 4.8. Here 'A' denotes Low SES Female respondents, 'B' denotes middle SES group and 'C' denotes high SES group.

On Deviant Behaviour means for three groups of female students are 4.21, 4.41 and 3.93 respectively. Difference is found to be significant for middle and high SES female students at .05 level.

For all other SSRVPs from V_1-V_{15} except Deviant Behaviour, the difference is found to be insignificant thus hypothesis is accepted which states that "There is no significant difference in sex and sexuality related values and perceptions among the females of low, middle and high SES level.

4.11. Interactional Effect of Sex and SES on SSRVPs of Adolescent Students

Values and perceptions related to sex and sexuality are a product of social, economic and personal condition in which individual lives. Zaidi (1988) notes that the relevance of certain notions, beliefs and attitudes motivate and promote adoption or act as negative motivating force in adoption of the values. To study the effect of sex and socio-economic status, ANOVA had been applied on 396 students. Table 4.9 presents the interactional effect of independent variables of sex and SES level on the Sex and sexuality related values and perceptions of the students.

Table 4.9

Interactional Effect of Sex and SES on SSRVPs of Adolescent Students

	Source of Variation	Sum of Squares	DF	Mean Square	F-ratio
V_1	Main effects	165.52	3	055.18	06.46**
	Sex	165.10	1	165.60	19.32**
	SES	001.94	2	000.97	00.11
	Two-way Interaction (Sex X SES)	011.93	2	005.97	00.69

V_2	Main effects	16.23	3	05.41	05.57**
	Sex	07.15	1	07.15	07.36
	SES	10.37	2	05.18	05.18
	Two-way Interaction (Sex X SES)	01.71	2	00.86	00.88
V_3	Main effects	02.10	3	00.70	02.51
	Sex	00.33	1	00.33	01.18
	SES	01.51	2	00.76	02.71
	Two-way Interaction (Sex X SES)	02.38	2	01.19	04.26*
V_4	Main effects	13.56	3	04.52	02.13
	Sex	00.25	1	00.25	00.12
	SES	12.68	2	06.34	02.99
	Two-way Interaction (Sex X SES)	02.23	2	01.11	05.24
V_5	Main effects	00.27	3	00.09	00.13
	Sex	00.08	1	00.08	00.12
	SES	00.22	2	00.11	00.16
	Two-way Interaction (Sex X SES)	00.65	2	00.33	00.48
V_6	Main effects	00.44	3	00.15	00.44
	Sex	00.38	1	00.38	01.12
	SES	00.10	2	00.05	00.15
	Two-way Interaction (Sex X SES)	00.96	2	00.48	01.44
V_7	Main effects	05.010	3	01.67	01.27
	Sex	02.570	1	02.57	01.96
	SES	03.180	2	01.59	01.21
	Two-way Interaction (Sex X SES)	00.912	2	00.46	00.35
V_8	Main effects	02.99	3	00.99	00.72
	Sex	00	1	00	00
	SES	02.97	2	01.49	01.07

	Two-way Interaction (Sex X SES)	04.41	2	02.21	01.59
V_9	Main effects	48.98	3	16.33	05.90**
	Sex	14.26	1	14.26	05.15*
	SES	30.11	2	15.05	05.44**
	Two-way Interaction (Sex X SES)	00.29	2	00.14	00.52
V_{10}	Main effects	14.68	3	04.89	01.14
	Sex	04.88	1	04.88	01.14
	SES	08.49	2	04.25	00.99
	Two-way Interaction (Sex X SES)	05.11	2	02.55	00.60
V_{11}	Main effects	01.15	3	00.38	00.37
	Sex	01.07	1	01.07	01.02
	SES	00.19	2	00.10	00.09
	Two-way Interaction (Sex X SES)	01.43	2	00.72	00.68
V_{12}	Main effects	07.89	3	02.63	02.11
	Sex	05.82	1	05.82	04.66*
	SES	02.58	2	01.29	01.03
	Two-way Interaction (Sex X SES)	01.86	2	00.93	00.74
V_{13}	Main effects	21.21	3	07.07	02.05
	Sex	15.89	1	15.89	04.61*
	SES	06.99	2	03.49	01.01
	Two-way Interaction (Sex X SES)	04.72	2	02.36	00.69
V_{14}	Main effects	07.54	3	02.51	02.41
	Sex	00.05	1	00.05	00.04
	SES	07.15	2	03.57	03.43*
	Two-way Interaction (Sex X SES)	00.91	2	00.45	00.44
V_{15}	Main effects	05.18	3	17.06	08.93**
	Sex	50.10	1	50.10	26.21**

SES	01.66	2	00.83	00.43
Two-way Interaction (Sex X SES)	00.92	2	00.46	00.24

* Significant at 0.05 level.
** Significant at 0.01 level.

To study the interactional effect of sex i.e. being male and female and low, middle or high SES on various SSRVPs (V_1 to V_{15}) ANOVA is applied as shown in Table 4.19.

On Homosexuality, interactional effect of sex and SES is showing a F-ratio as 4.26 which is significant at .05 level. It shows that Homosexuality is significantly affected by the interactional effect of sex and SES of the subjects.

Other than Homosexuality all values snow insignificant F-ratios to mean that there is no significant interactional effect of sex and SES on the students's sex and sexuality related values and perceptions thus accepting the hypothesis No.9 which states *"There is no interactional effect of sex and SES on sex and sexuality related values and perceptions of students"*.

Part III

As per the objectives, the study of Sex and sexuality related values and perceptions of teachers has been put in Part III of this chapter. The requisite information from teachers is collected on the questionnaire developed by the researcher. 45 items relating to values and perceptions of questionnaire belong to 15 components of Sex and sexuality education. Its details have been given in Chapter 3. As per the design of study to make inter-group comparisons on sex and grades of teachers, t-test has been applied. In order to make inter group comparison Duncan's Range Test has been applied and to see the interactional effect of sex and grades on Sex and sexuality related values and perceptions ANOVA has been applied. Results are given in the tables from 4.10 to 4.16.

4.12 Comparison of Sex and Sexuality Related Values and Perceptions between TGT & PGT Teachers

83 PGT teachers and 61 PGT teachers had given their responses on 45 items in the questionnaire which have been clubbed in 15 components as they have been described in Chapter 3.

Mean and standard deviation for the two grades of teachers and 't' values have been given in the following table

Table 4.10

Mean SSRVPs Scores and Standard Deviation and Results of t-test between TGT and PGT Grade Teachers

	TGT (N= 83)		PGT (N= 61)		
Value	**Mean**	**SD**	**Mean**	**SD**	**t-value**
V_1	23.02	03.08	22.97	02.58	00.12
V_2	07.82	01.33	08.26	00.99	02.19*
V_3	02.84	00.43	02.90	00.35	00.90
V_4	07.74	01.26	07.92	01.26	00.86
V_5	02.53	00.83	02.34	00.87	01.30
V_6	02.83	00.51	02.93	00.36	01.34
V_7	05.65	00.79	05.57	01.01	00.51
V_8	04.02	01.46	03.57	01.67	01.72
V_9	09.58	01.84	09.48	01.69	00.34
V_{10}	15.55	02.16	16.34	01.76	02.34*

V_{11}	05.55	00.85	05.75	00.65	01.54
V_{12}	04.98	01.17	05.21	00.97	01.22
V_{13}	11.09	01.99	11.34	01.91	00.7
V_{14}	03.75	00.87	03.74	00.89	00.06
V_{15}	03.65	01.45	03.16	01.09	02.20*

* Significant at 0.05 level

This is evident from the above Table 4.10 that for components Gender Equality, Role of Religion and Morality and Heterosexuality, a significant difference is found between teacher of TGT and PGT grades at 0.05 level. Such results are discussed below:

Mean values for Gender Equality are 7.82, 8.26 and SD was 1.33 and 0.99 for TGTs and PGTs respectively. t-value is found to be 2.19 which shows that TGTs and PGTs are significantly different at .05 level. On the component Gender Equality PGT grade teachers have higher mean value as 8.26 showing more favour for Gender Equality.

In case teachers, on 'Role of Religion and Morality' mean and SD values are 15.55 and 2.16 for TGTs while 16.34 and 1.76 in case of PGTs. t-value is 2.34 which is found to be significant at .05 level. Higher mean value in case of PGTs shows they are in more agreement with values relating to 'Role of Religion and Morality'.

Mean values for 'Heterosexuality' are 3.65 and 3.16 and SD values as 1.45 and 1.09 for TGTs and PGTs respectively. t-value of 2.20 is found to show significant difference at 0.05 level between two groups of TGT and PGT.

The components V_1 – Need for Sex Education, V_3 - Homosexuality, V_4 - Virginity, V_5 Peer Group

Dependence V_6 - Monogamy, V_7 Role of Media, V_8 - Deviant Behaviour, V_9 - Social Approval, V_{11} - Sex Crime, V_{12} - Life Style, V_{13} - Dating, V_{15} - Myths and Misconceptions are found to have insignificant t-values and hence there is no difference between two groups of TGT and PGT on these values. This shows that Hypothesis 10 has been accepted for these sex and sexuality related values and perceptions.

4.13 Comparison of Sex and Sexuality Related Values and Perceptions between TGT Male and PGT Male Teachers

15 male TGT teachers and 15 male PGT teachers had given their responses on 45 items in the questionnaire which have been clubbed in 15 components denoted as V_1 to V_{15} as described in table 4.11.

Table 4.11

Mean SSRVPs Scores, SDs and results of t-test between MaleTGT and PGT Grade Teachers

	TGT Male Teahers (N= 15)		PGT Male Teahers (N= 15)		t-value
Value	**Mean**	**SD**	**Mean**	**SD**	
V_1	24.00	02.88	22.07	02.66	01.91
V_2	07.33	01.29	07.93	01.16	01.34
V_3	02.87	00.35	02.93	00.26	00.59
V_4	07.67	01.59	07.93	01.83	00.43
V_5	02.33	00.98	02.47	00.83	00.40
V_6	02.53	00.83	03.00	00	
V_7	05.67	01.05	05.07	01.69	01.18
V_8	04.07	01.67	03.53	01.64	00.88
V_9	08.13	01.99	08.07	01.39	00.11

V_{10}	14.73	03.26	16.40	01.404	01.82
V_{11}	05.67	00.62	06.00	00	-
V_{12}	04.40	01.50	05.13	00.83	01.65
V_{13}	10.67	02.09	11.80	01.21	01.82
V_{14}	03.33	00.90	03.47	01.19	00.35
V_{15}	04.33	01.35	03.27	01.10	02.38*

* Significant at 0.05 level.

To compare the two groups of male teachers on Sex and sexuality related values and perceptions t-test is applied which shows that on the component 'Heterosexuality' the mean values are 4.33 and 3.27 respectively for TGT Male teachers and male teachers and SDs for them are 1.35 and 1.1. t-value is 2.38 which is significant at 0.05 level. For all other values under components V_1 - V_{14}, the difference is insignificant.

This means that only for the component V_{15} – Heterosexuality, Hypothesis No.11 *"There is no significant difference on sex related values and perceptions of TGT male and PGT male teachers"* is rejected.

For components V_1-V_{14}, the Hypothesis is accepted.

4.14. Comparison of Sex and Sexuality Related Values and Perceptions between Female TGT and PGT Grade Teachers

68 female TGT grade teachers and 46 female PGT grade teachers had given their responses on 45 items in the questionnaire which have been clubbed in 15 components denoted as V_1 to V_{15}.

Mean, standard deviation and t-value for the female teachers have been given in the table 4.12.

Table 4.12

Mean SSRVPs Scores, SDs and results of t-test between Female TGT and PGT Grade Teachers

	TGT Teachers (N= 68)		PGT Teachers (N= 46)		
Value	**Mean**	**SD**	**Mean**	**SD**	**t-value**
V_1	22.81	03.10	23.26	02.51	00.82
V_2	07.93	01.32	08.37	00.93	01.97
V_3	02.84	00.44	02.89	00.38	00.66
V_4	07.75	01.19	07.91	01.03	00.76
V_5	02.37	00.79	02.30	00.89	01.69
V_6	02.89	00.39	02.91	00.41	00.21
V_7	05.69	00.73	05.74	00.61	00.71
V_8	04.02	01.42	03.59	01.69	01.46
V_9	09.89	01.65	09.94	01.54	00.12
V_{10}	15.74	01.82	16.33	01.87	01.68
V_{11}	05.53	00.89	05.67	00.73	00.91
V_{12}	05.12	01.06	05.24	01.02	00.61
V_{13}	11.19	01.97	11.19	02.07	00.01
V_{14}	03.84	00.84	03.83	00.77	00.08
V_{15}	03.50	01.44	03.13	01.11	01.47

On perusal of the table 4.12, it is evident that female TGT and PGT grade teachers do not significantly from each other on any of the variables i.e. from V_1 to V_{15}. Hence, hypothesis no.12 has been retained which states *"There is no significant difference in sex and sexuality related values and perceptions of female TGT and PGT grade teachers"*.

4.15. Comparison of Mean Scores and SDs for Male and Female Teachers (TGT) on Sex and Sexuality Related Values and Perceptions

68 female and 15 male TGT teachers had given their responses on 45 items in the questionnaire which have been grouped in 15 components denoted as V_1 to V_{15}.

Mean, standard deviation and t-value for the TGT grade teachers have been given in the following table.

Table 4.13

Mean SSRVPs Scores and results of t-test between Male and Female TGT Grade Teachers

	Female TGT (N= 68)		Male PGT (N= 15)		
Value	**Mean**	**SD**	**Mean**	**SD**	**t-value**
V_1	22.81	03.10	24.00	02.88	01.36
V_2	07.93	01.32	07.33	01.29	01.60
V_3	02.84	00.44	02.87	00.35	00.23
V_4	07.75	01.19	07.67	01.59	00.23
V_5	02.57	00.79	02.33	00.98	01.01
V_6	02.89	00.39	02.53	00.83	02.57**
V_7	05.65	00.73	05.67	01.05	00.09
V_8	04.02	01.42	04.07	01.67	00.12
V_9	09.89	01.65	08.13	01.99	03.61**
V_{10}	15.74	01.82	14.73	03.26	01.64
V_{11}	05.53	00.89	05.67	00.62	00.57
V_{12}	05.12	01.06	04.40	01.50	02.19*
V_{13}	11.19	01.97	10.67	02.09	00.92
V_{14}	03.84	00.84	03.33	00.90	02.08*
V_{15}	03.50	01.44	04.33	01.35	02.14*

* Significant at 0.05 level.

** Significant at 0.01 level.

When one looks at table No.4.13, it is visible that significant differences are found in the values and perceptions about sex and sexuality among male and female TGT grade teachers relating to components V_6 (Monogamy), V_9 (Social Approval), V_{12} (Life Style), V_{14} (Myths and Misconceptions) and V_{15} (Heterosexuality) at 0.05 or 0.01 levels. The details of these are given below:

Mean values on V_6 'Monogamy' are 2.90 for female and 2.53 for male TGT teachers. SDs are 0.39 and 0.83 for the two groups respectively. t-value is 2.57 which is significant at 0.01 level implying that female have favoured Monogamy more than male counterparts. The same finding has been reported by Kala's (1995) which concludes that Indian traditional value of one sexual married partner is of great value in the era of HIV/AIDs.

Results of the research on both normative and personal standards toward extramarital sexuality indicate that, overall, most people in Western cultures disapproves of extramarital sexuality in general and for the self (e.g. Glenn & Weaver, 1979; Klemmack & Roff, 1980; Lawson & Samson, 1988; Reiss, Anderson & Sponaugle, 1980; Singh, Walton, & Williams, 1976). For example, from 1980 national data (Davis, 1980), 4% of American adults felt that extramarital sex was never wrong, and 70% felt that it was always wrong. From responses to the General Social Survey in 1988 (greeley, 1991), 86% of American adults said that marital infidelity (sexual relations with someone other than the marriage partner) was always wrong or almost always wrong.

We have limited information on attitudes toward other extradyadic relationships (sexual relationships outside of committed but non-marital relationships).

As part of a larger study of homosexual and heterosexual couples, Kurdek (1991b) compared the attitudes toward sexual fidelity of several subgroups. He reported that gay couples value fidelity significantly less than lesbian or heterosexual couples. Peplau and Cochran (1981) reported that sexual exclusively in relationships was rated as more important by heterosexuals than by a matched group of homosexuals. However, most homosexuals, like heterosexuals, do value or prefer steady, love relationships (bell & Weinberg, 1978; Peplau & Gordon, 1983).

Sponaugle (1989) reported that greater acceptance of extramarital sexuality is related to being male, holding more permissive premarital standards, lower marital satisfaction and marital sexual satisfaction, higher educational attainment, lower religiosity, perceived opportunity for extramarital activity, greater gender equality, higher liberalism, and being unmarried. In an earlier review, Thompson (1983) argued that pre-marital sexual standrds are the best predictor of extramarital sexual standards, probably because both premarital and extramarital permissiveness are influenced by some of the same factors, such as gender, race, and general liberalism. Reiss et al. (1980), from an analysis of survey data from representative samples of adults obtained by the National Opinion Research Center (NORC), also found that premarital sexual permissiveness, along with marital satisfaction, was a key predictor of extramarital permissiveness.

Bower and Chiristopher (1977) found that college students generally were approving of cohabitation as long as no children were involved and the couple was monogamous. Sixty percent of these students felt that cohabitation was appropriate in order to try out a relationship.

In a late 1970s poll of American adults (MsClosky & Brill, 1983), 46% of the sample said living together was morally wrong, Wiersma (1983) studied a probability sample of American adults who were cohabiting, and 72% of this group said their relatives and friends had some concerns about their cohabitation relationship. Finally, in a more recent study analyzing data from the National Survey of Families and Households (Sweet, Bumpass, & Call, 1988), respondents who were unmarried and younger than 36 years old were asked about their attitudes toward cohabitation. Of these respondents, 35% indicated a definite desire to live with someone without being married to find out whether they would be compatible for marriage, and 51% said it would be all right for them to do so.

For V_9 - 'Social Approval', the mean values for female TGTs is 9.89 and 8.13 for male TGTs. SD is 1.65 and 1.99 respectively. t-value comes out as 3.61 which shows the difference here is highly significant at .01 level.

For component 'Life Style' mean values are 5.12 and 4.40 for female TGT and male TGTs. SDs are calculated as 1.06 and 1.50 respectively. t-value of 2.19 shows the two groups of TGT and PGT are significantly different on Life Style

On Myths and Misconceptions mean values are 3.84 and 3.33 for female TGT and female TGT respectively. SD comes out to be 0.84 and 0.90

respectively. T-value is 2.08 which is showing significant difference between them at .05 level.

Observing the table 5.4,for V_{15} Heterosexuality mean value is 3.50 & 4.33 for female and male TGTs respectively. SD is 1.44 and 1.35 for female and male teachers (TGTs). t-value is 2.14 which shows that the difference between two groups to be significant at .05 level for Heterosexuality.

In all other values relating to components V_1 - Need for Sex Education, V_2 - Gender Equality, V_3 - Homosexuality, V_4 - Virginity, V_5 - Peer Group Dependence, V_7 - Role of Media, V_8 - Deviant Behaviour, V_{10} - Role of Religion and Morality, V_{11} - Sex Crime, and V_{13} Dating no significant different is found between female and male TGT grade teachers. hence, the hypothesis 13 which states *"There is no significant difference in sex and sexuality related values and perceptions of male and female TGT grade teachers"* is retained for the above mentioned components.

4.16. Comparison of Mean Scores and SDs of Male and Female Teachers of PGT grade on Sex and Sexuality Related Values and Perceptions

46 female and 15 male PGT teachers had given their responses on 45 items in the questionnaire which have been grouped in 15 components denoted as V_1 to V_{15}. Mean, standard deviation and t-value for the PGT grade teachers have been given in the table 4.14.

As is evident from the above table, only on the component V_7 – Role of Media and V_9 – Social Approval, a significant difference is seen between the male and female PGT grade teachers at .05 level and .01 level respectively.

Table 4.14

Mean SSRVPs Scores SDs and results of t-test between Male and Female PGT Grade Teachers

	PGT Female (N= 46)		PGT Male (N= 15)		
Value	**Mean**	**SD**	**Mean**	**SD**	**t-value**
V_1	23.26	02.51	22.07	02.66	01.58
V_2	08.37	00.93	07.93	01.16	01.48
V_3	02.89	00.38	02.93	00.26	00.40
V_4	07.91	01.03	07.93	01.83	00.05
V_5	02.30	00.89	02.47	00	00.62
V_6	02.91	00.41	03.00	01.67	
V_7	05.74	00.61	05.07	01.64	02.33*
V_8	03.59	01.69	03.53	01.40	00.11
V_9	09.94	01.54	08.07	01.40	04.41**
V_{10}	16.33	01.87	16.40	01.40	00.14
V_{11}	05.67	00.73	06.00	00.00	
V_{12}	05.24	01.02	05.13	00.83	00.36
V_{13}	11.19	02.07	11.80	01.21	01.07
V_{14}	03.83	00.77	03.47	01.19	01.36
V_{15}	03.13	01.11	03.27	01.10	00.41

* Significant at .05 level

** Significant at .01 level

\- value not significant.

On 'Role of Media' mean values are 5.74 and 5.07 for PGT Female and PGT Male respectively. SD is 0.61 and 1.67 respectively. t-value is found to be 2.33 is significant at .05 level. However, Rao (1976) found in the similiar type of study that majority of teachers of both genders favoured sex education in schools and media could play significant role in it. Similar opinion has been given by Yang (1988) where he examined causes of moral control and revealed that media has created such an atmosphere which appears to encourage sex and permissive attitude.

For the component 'Social Approval' mean values are 9.94 and 8.07 respectively. SDs are 1.54 and 1.40. t-value is 4.41 which shows difference to be significant at .01 level. Mata Ragnon (1982) found in Philippines that there prevailed double standards on the matters of social permissions.

For other components namely V_1 - Need for Sex Education, V_2 - Gender Equality, V_3 - Homosexuality, V_4 - Virginity, V_5 - Peer Group Dependence, V_6 - Monogamy, V_8 - Deviant Behaviour, V_{10} - Role of Religion and Morality, V_{11} - Sex Crime, V_{12} - Life Style, V_{13} - Dating, V_{14} - Myths and Misconceptions, V_{15} - Heterosexuality no significant difference between these groups are found thus hypothesis 16 is relevant for these components which states as – There is no significant difference in sex and sexuality related values and perceptions of male and female PGT grade teachers.

4.17 Comparison of Male and Female Teachers of both PGT and TGT grades where TGT Female=A, PGT Female=B, TGT Male=C, PGT Male=D

(Duncan's Range Test}

To make intergroup comparisons between two genders of TGT and PGT grade teachers Duncan's Range Test has been applied. Their means have been compared to find out significant relationship between them. The results have been shown in table 4.15.

Table 4.15

Mean Scores of SSRVPs at TGT and PGT Grade Male and Female Teachers and result of Duncan's Range Test

Variable	TGT (F)	PGT (F)	TGT (M)	PGT (M)	Significantly Different Groups					
	A (N=68)	B (N=46)	C (N=15)	D (N=15)	A/B	A/C	A/D	B/C	B/D	C/D
V_1	20.81	23.26	24.00	22.07	-	-	-	-	-	-
V_2	07.93	08.37	07.33	07.93	-	-	-	*	-	-
V_3	02.84	02.89	02.87	02.93	-	-	-	-	-	-
V_4	07.75	07.91	07.67	07.93	-	-	-	-	-	-
V_5	02.57	02.30	02.33	02.47	-	-	-	-	-	-
V_6	02.90	02.91	02.53	03.00	-	*	-	*	-	*
V_7	05.65	05.74	05.67	05.07	-	-	*	-	*	-
V_8	04.01	03.59	04.07	03.53	-	-	-	-	-	-
V_9	09.90	09.93	08.13	08.07	-	*	*	*	*	-

Variable	TGT (F)	PGT (F)	TGT (M)	PGT (M)	Significantly Different Groups					
	A	B	C	D	A/B	A/C	A/D	B/C	B/D	C / D
	(N=68)	(N=46)	(N=15)	(N=15)						
V_{10}	15.74	16.33	14.73	16.40	-	-	-	*	-	*
V_{11}	05.53	05.67	05.67	06.00	-	-	*	-	-	-
V_{12}	05.12	05.24	04.40	05.13	-	*	-	*	-	-
V_{13}	11.19	11.20	10.67	11.80	-	-	-	-	-	-
V_{14}	03.84	03.83	10.67	03.47	-	-	-	-	-	-
V_{15}	03.50	03.13	03.33	03.27	-	*	-	*	-	*

*Significant at 0.05 level.

-Not significant.

Four groups comprised of TGT female (N=68), PGT female (N=46), TGT male (N=15) and PGT males (N=15). V_1 - On Need for Sex Education, all the teachers have shown high mean value of 22.81, 23.26, 24.00 and 22.07. It could be inferred from their findings that they favour integration of Sex Education in Schools which is not so in the findings of Pohlman, Edward and Rao (1970). As per their findings teachers of both Genders did not advocate Sex Education at primary or secondary level. Similarly Maheshwari (1972) also found that teachers from South Delhi are against introduction of sex education in schools. However, as per the findings of survey by Ministry of Education, Culture and Sports, Manila (1973) majority of teachers favoured introduction of Sex Education and Reproduction related issues in the School Curriculum.

Component 'Gender Equality', shows mean values as 7.93, 8.37, 7.33 and 7.93, respectively for TGT female, PGT female, TGT male and PGT male teachers.

PGT female teachers differed significantly from TGT males on this value i.e. Gender Equality. Other groups show no significant difference with each other.

For component 'Monogamy' mean value for TGT female, PGT female, TGT male, PGT male is found to be 2.90, 2.91, 2.53 and 3.00 respectively. TGT female and TGT female show significant difference at .05 level. PGT male and PGT male show significant difference at 0.05 level. TGT (M) and PGT (M) show significant difference at 0.05 level.

The effects of media violence have been vigorously debated for several decades. Televised violence is of special concern because of its vivid and realistic nature and its easy accessibility to children. Social scientists disagree on whether there is enough evidence of antisocial effects of violence or pornography to justify censorship. Many social scientists insist that Constitution places a strong burden of proof on the censor, that a much stronger case cold be made for censorship of violence including violent pornography) than of nonviolent pornography, and that attempts to censor media content because it is alleged to produce "bad attitudes" are in conflect with the free marketplace of ideas model assumed by the Constitution.

While social scientists see media violence as more harmful than pornography, the need for censorship of nonviolent pornography more than of violence is the common view. This suggests that people underestimate the effects of media violence, overestimate the effects of nonviolent pornography, or object to pornography for reasons other than its alleged harmful effects.

The effects of violent pornography can be explained by the same theories that explained by the same theories that explain the effects of general film violence. Those who claim that nonviolent pornography causes aggression are faced with the problem of explaining how nonaggressive content (sexuality) can activate aggressive behaviour. A variation on arousal theory, the excitation transfer theory, suggests that the physiological arousal caused by pornography can subsequently be confused with anger and can energize aggression. Any source of arousal, such as music or exercise, can have this effect if the timing is right. This theory predicts very subtle, temporary effects of exposure to pornography, and as noted, research does not consistently support it.

Effects of aggression and pornography on attitudes can be explained on the basis of theories of attitude change, which show that, non surprisingly, almost any media presentation produces small, temporary changes of attitude in the direction advocated by its author. Resistance to attitude change occurs when the audience has the information and the motivation to argue with the media effectively.

For 'Role of Media' mean value for the above mentioned four groups are 5.65, 5.74, 5.67 and 5.07, respectively. Difference between the following groups of teachers is found to be significant at .05 level.

TGT female and PGT male, PGT male and PGT female

On value Social Approval mean value came out to be 9.90, 9.93, 8.13 and 8.07 respectively for TGT female, PGT female, TGT male and PGT male. Following groups are found to be significantly different at .05 level, TGT female and TGT male, TGT female and PGT male, PGT female and TGT male, PGT female and PGT male. Rest of the groups are found not to be significantly different from each other. Comparison of four groups on component 'Role of Religion and Morality' that shows a means of 15.74, 16.33, 14.73 and 16.40 respectively for the four groups.

Following groups shows significant differences among them at 0.05 level:

PGT female and TGT male, TGT male and PGT male.

Following table 4.15 for the component V_{11} - 'Sex Crime' shows the mean values for four groups on 5.53, 5.67, 5.67 and 6.0 respectively. TGT (F) and PGT (M) teachers show the difference between them to be significant at 0.05 level other groups do not show significant difference between them on this component. Perusal of table (Duncan's Range Test) 4.15 shows that mean value on value Heterosexuality is 3.50, 3.13, 4.33 and 3.27 respectively, for above mentioned four groups. Following groups are found to differ significantly at 0.05 level on Heterosexuality. TGT female and TGT male,

PGT female and TGT male, TGT male and PGT male

The components Need for Sex Education, Homosexuality, Virginity, Peer Group Dependence, Deviant Behaviour, Dating, Myths and Misconceptions are found to have no significant difference among any of the four conditions hence retaining the hypothesis No.15 for these components, which states *"There is no significant difference in sex and sexuality related values and perceptions of male and female teachers of both PGT and TGT grades"*.

4.18. Interactional Effect of Independent Variables and Sex and Grades on Dependent Variables of SSRVPs

Values and perceptions related to sex and sexuality are a product of social, economic and personal condition in which individual lives. Zaidi (1988) opined that the relevance of certain notions, beliefs and attitudes motivate and promote adoption or act as negative motivating force in adoption of the values. To study the effect of sex and being TGT or PGT on Sex and sexuality related values and perceptions of teachers, ANOVA had been applied on respondents 144 teachers. Table 4.16 presented the interactional effect on Sex and sexuality related values and perceptions of two dependent variables of sex and grades. Interactional effect has been seen for V_1 to V_{15}, each variable separately as presented below:

Table 4.16

Interactional Effect of Sex (Male & Female) and Group (TGT and PGT) on Sex and Sexuality Related Values and Perceptions (ANOVA) (N=144)

	Source of Variation	Sum of Squares	DF	Mean Square	F-ratio
V_1	Main Effect	00.17	2	00.08	00.01
	Sex (M, F)	00.05	1	00.05	00.01
	Group (TGT, PGT)	00.13	1	00.13	00.02
	Two-way interaction (Sex X Group)	33.51	1	33.51	04.12*
V_2	Main Effect	13.23	2	06.62	04.69**
	Sex	06.33	1	06.33	04.49*
	Group	07.94	1	07.94	05.63*
	Two-way interaction	00.15	1	00.15	00.10
V_3	Main Effect	00.15	2	00.07	00.46
	Sex	00.03	1	00.03	00.18
	Group	00.11	1	00.11	00.69
	Two-way interaction	00.001	1	.001	00.01
V_4	Main Effect	01.21	2	00.60	00.38
	Sex	00.03	1	00.03	00.02
	Group	01.20	1	01.20	00.75
	Two-way interaction	00.06	1	00.06	00.04

V_5	Main Effect	01.27	2	00.63	00.88
	Sex	00.05	1	00.05	00.07
	Group	01.17	1	01.17	01.61
	Two-way interaction	00.95	1	00.95	01.32
V_6	Main Effect	00.89	2	00.44	02.45
	Sex	00.52	1	00.52	02.61
	Group	00.44	1	00.44	02.25
	Two-way interaction	01.20	1	01.20	06.05*
V_7	Main Effect	02.51	2	01.25	01.65
	Sex	02.30	1	02.30	03.02
	Group	00.11	1	00.11	00.15
	Two-way interaction	02.82	1	02.82	03.70
V_8	Main Effect	07.13	2	03.57	01.47
	Sex	00	1	000	000
	Group	07.09	1	07.09	02.91
	Two-way interaction	00.07	1	00.07	00.03
V_9	Main Effect	78.01	2	39.01	14.69**
	Sex	77.64	1	77.64	29.24**
	Group	00.01	2	00.01	00.003
	Two-way interaction	00.06	1	00.06	00.024
V_{10}	Main Effect	27.53	2	13.76	03.47
	Sex	05.58	1	05.58	01.41
	Group	23.59	1	23.59	05.94*
	Two-way interaction	06.82	1	06.82	01.72
V_{11}	Main Effect	02.63	2	01.31	02.23
	Sex	01.22	1	01.22	02.08
	Group	01.20	1	01.20	02.03
	Two-way interaction	00.21	1	00.21	00.36

V_{12}	Main Effect	06.03	2	03.02	02.60
	Sex	04.25	1	04.25	03.66
	Group	02.23	1	02.23	01.92
	Two-way interaction	02.21	1	02.21	01.90
V_{13}	Main Effect	02.17	2	1.003	00.28
	Sex	00.01	1	00.01	00.002
	Group	02.13	1	02.13	00.56
	Two-way interaction	07.51	1	07.51	01.96
V_{14}	Main Effect	04.47	2	02.24	02.99*
	Sex	04.47	1	04.47	05.97*
	Group	00.01	1	00.01	00.02
	Two-way interaction	00.13	1	00.13	00.17
V_{15}	Main Effect	14.21	2	07.11	04.21*
	Sex	05.88	1	05.88	03.48
	Group	09.42	1	09.42	05.58*
	Two-way interaction	02.86	1	02.86	01.70

*Significant at 0.05 level.

**Significant at 0.01 level.

The table 4.16 shows that for Values and Perceptions under component V_1 'Need for Sex Education', F-ratio of main effect, sex and group are 0.01, 0.01 and 0.02 which are not significant. Interactional Effect for Need for Sex Education shows F-ratio of 4.12 which is significant at 0.05 level. For V_6 'Monogamy' interactional effect of sex and group (TGT/PGT) on Sex and sexuality related values and perceptions has F-ratio of 6.05 which is also significant at 0.05 level. The results of these two components V_1 and V_6 show that being male or female and being at PGT or TGT grade did affect the responses of teachers for the variable 'Need for Sex Education' and 'Monogamy'

For variables Homosexuality, Virginity, Peer Group Dependence, Role of Media, Deviant Behaviour, Social Approval, Role of Religion and Morality, Sex Crime, Life Style, Dating and Heterosexuality, the hypothesis No.16 *"There is no interactional effect of sex and being TGT, PGT on the Sex and sexuality related values and perceptions of teachers"*, is retained.

5

Conclusions, Educational Implications and Suggestions for Further Research

5.1 Introduction

This chapter first presents the conclusions arrived at as a result of analysis and interpretations of data, after that educational implications of the findings of the study have been discussed. At the end, a few possible problems on which further research may be conducted have been suggested.

5.2 Conclusions

The main objectives of the study are - to study the sex and sexuality related values and perceptions of students and teachers belonging to two sexes and socio-economic status grades.

For knowing the sex and sexuality related values and perceptions, a tool having 45 items was prepared by the researcher. They were grouped into the following 15 components/variables.

V_1	Need for Sex Education
V_2	Gender Equality
V_3	Homosexuality
V_4	Virginity
V_5	Peer Group Dependence
V_6	Monogamy
V_7	Role of Media
V_8	Deviant Behaviour
V_9	Social Approval
V_{10}	Role of Religion and Morality
V_{11}	Sex Crime
V_{12}	Lifestyle
V_{13}	Dating
V_{14}	Myths and Misconceptions
V_{15}	Heterosexuality

Validity and reliability of the tool were established. The tool was administered on a sample of 396 students and 144 teachers. To determine the SES of students, a tool prepared by Hasnain and Srivastava (1999) was used. SES scale provided low, middle and high SES levels of students. The scores achieved on SSRVPs scale by the respondents were tabulated and analysed statistically. The results so obtained were interpreted. For the students mean, standard deviation, t-test and Duncan's Range test were applied. To know the interactional effect of Sex and SES on the SSRVPs of students ANOVA was applied. For teacher respondents mean standard deviation, and Duncan's Range test was applied. To know the interactional effect of Sex and Grades ANOVA was applied.

Major Findings

The major findings of the results so obtained have been given below:

1. For the components/variables of sex and sexuality related values and perceptions viz. gender equality, peer group dependence, monogamy, social approval and dating and values and perceptions covered under these components, the hypothesis which states that "there is no significant difference between sex and sexuality related values and perceptions of adolescent students and their teachers", is retained.

   While for the components: Need for Sex Education, Homosexuality, Virginity, Role of Media, Deviant Behaviour, Role of Religion and Morality, Sex Crime, Life Style, Myths and Misconceptions and Heterosexuality, the hypothesis is rejected. The difference on these components has been found significant either on 0.01 or 0.05 level.

2. There is a significant difference between male and female adolescent students in values and perceptions relating to the need for sex education, gender equality, social approval, life styles and heterosexuality. But for components: Homosexuality, Virginity, Peer Group Dependence, Monogamy, Role of Media, Deviant behaviour, Role of Religion and Morality, Dating and Myths and Misconceptions, the difference is not significant.

3. Comparison of the three groups of adolescent students belonging to low, middle and high SES levels is found to be insignificantly different on values and perceptions of the components - Peer Group

Dependence, Monogamy, Role of Media, Deviant Behaviour, Role of Religion and Morality, Sex Crime, Life Style, Dating and Heterosexuality.

However, a significant difference is visible between high SES students differ from middle and low SES adolescence students on values and perceptions relating to gender equality. For the component, homosexuality, there is a significant difference between low SES group vs. middle and high SES group, where low SES group has lower mean value for it. A significant difference is also found between low SES group and high SES group for the component virginity where high SES group holds this value more strongly.

Between low SES group and high SES group and also between middle SES group and high SES group, there is a significant difference found in values and perceptions relating to the variable social approval. For the component 'Myths and Misconceptions', there is a significant difference between values and perceptions of low and middle SES group. Middle SES students show less agreement on myths and misconceptions that are prevalent.

4. On variables, gender equality, virginity, peer group dependence, monogamy, role of media, deviant behaviour, social approval, role of religion and morality, sex crime, lifestyle, myths and misconceptions, no significant difference is found between male and female adolescent students of low SES

group. But there is a significant difference between male and female adolescent students of low SES group in the values and perceptions relating to need for sex education, homosexuality, dating and heterosexuality. Male students show more agreement on these values except homosexuality.

5. Male and female adolescent students of middle SES level have a significant difference in values and perceptions relating to the variables need for sex education and 'heterosexuality'. For other components, the difference is insignificant. Male students show higher agreement on these value statements.

6. Comparison of sex and sexuality related values and perceptions of male and female adolescent students of high SES showed the difference to be significant at gender equality variable and heterosexuality. The difference was insignificant on other variables. Here male students show more agreement on their value statements.

7. Comparison of male students of different SES shows significant difference on the values and perceptions relating to Gender Equality, homosexuality, virginity, social approval and myths and misconceptions. High SES males agree more on Gender Equality and social approval than the middle or low SES males. The difference was insignificant among the male students of low, middle and high SES on Need for Sex Education, Peer Group Dependence,

Monogamy, Role of Media, Deviant Behaviour, Role of Religion and Morality, Sex Crime, Life Style, Dating, and Heterosexuality components.

8. Comparison of female students of low, middle and high SES shows no significant difference among them on values and perceptions relating to all the variables except that of the variable Deviant behaviour where a significant difference is seen between middle and high SES groups. Middle class females agree more on these value components.
9. There was no interactional effect of sex and SES on sex and sexuality related values and perceptions of students except on the component of homosexuality where the interactional effect of sex and SES on sex and sexuality related values and perceptions was significant.
10. Comparison of sex and sexuality related values and perceptions of TGT and PGT showed the difference to be significant on sex and sexuality related values and perceptions relating to the components of gender equality, role of religion and morality and heterosexuality. On Need for Sex Education, Homosexuality, Virginity, Peer Group Dependence, Monogamy, Role of Media, Deviant Behaviour, Social Approval, Sex Crime, Life Style, Dating, Myths and Misconceptions there was no significant difference between TGT and PGT grade teachers.
11. On comparison of male TGT and PGT grade

teachers, difference is found to be significant on the sex and sexuality related values and perceptions relating to heterosexuality. On all other variables, there is no significant difference hence accepting the hypothesis that there is no significant difference between males of two grades of teachers.

12. There is no significant difference in values and perceptions relating to sex and sexuality between female teachers of two grades.

13. Comparison of male and female teachers of TGT grade shows no significant difference between their sex and sexuality related values and perceptions relating to variables Need for Sex Education, Gender Equality, Homosexuality, Virginity, Peer Group Dependence, Role of Media, Deviant Behaviour, Role of Religion and Morality, Sex Crime and Dating. However, significant difference is seen for variables Monogamy, Social Approval, Life Style, Myths and Misconceptions and Heterosexuality. Higher agreement on these value components is shown by female TGTs except Heterosexuality value.

14. Comparison of male and female teachers of PGT grades shows the difference to be significant on role of media and social approval. There is no significant difference in values and perceptions relating to other components.

15. Values and perceptions relating to components Need for Sex Education,

Homosexuality, Virginity, Peer Group Dependence, Deviant Behaviour, Dating, and Myths and Misconceptions are found to have no significant difference among male and female teachers of TGT and PGT grade. However, female and male PGT differ on Gender Equality and higher agreement shown by female PGTs. Female and male TGT. Female and male PGT and male TGT and PGT differ on Monogamy. Female TGT and male PGT, female and male PGT differ on Role of Media. On Social Approval, the difference is found to be significant among female and male TGT, female TGT and male PGT, female PGT and male TGT and female PGT and male PGT. There is a significant difference in sex and sexuality related values and perceptions related to the variable 'Role of Religion' and 'Morality' among female PGT and male TGT and male TGT and male PGT. For Sex Crime, female TGT and male PGT differ significantly. In case of Life Style, a significant difference is found among female TGT and male TGT, female PGT and male TGT. Also for the component 'Heterosexuality', there is a significant difference between female TGT and male TGT, female PGT and male TGT and male TGT and male PGT. Higher agreement is shown by TGT grade females on this component.

16. Except for the component, need for sex education and monogamy, there is no significant interactional effect of sex and being TGT/PGT on the sex and sexuality

related values and perceptions relating to other components.

5.3 Educational Implications

The importance of any piece of research in education lies in the implications of the findings of the study. This is how, the research findings of a study can be made useful. Population education must be viewed as an important part of nation's strategy to contain the growth of populations. UNFPA, Director Nafis Sadik endorses the view saying that, "There is only one acceptable way to slow down population growth and that is through freedom of choice. That means paying attention to the individual needs, reproductive health, education and equality between women and men. Freedom to choose is influenced by the basic set of values and knowledge possessed by the individual". Adolescence education's one of the aims is training in sexuality and reproductive values as emphasised by NPE, 1986. The findings of the study may help in organising such training as it covers both teacher and student perspectives.

From the survey of researches, conducted in the field of population education in India, it is revealed that the field of sex education has been touched by very few researches. A complete sketch of human values and perceptions related to sex and sexuality as delineated by this study would help the policy planners and curriculum framers in the field of population/adolescence/sex education.

The problem of immoral sexual behaviour, sex crime on increase and adoption of M TV culture/ influence of western culture through satellite TV by the students has created an alarming situation. This problem is becoming grave not only in our country but the whole world is in its grip. It has drawn attention of researchers and needs immediate action that should be based on the research findings.

Most of the developed countries have started imparting sex education. In India many institutions have accepted sex education programmes with various focusses and under different connotations. However, it still awaits for its due in formal education system. The findings of this study would help in devising a curriculum and approach to sex education.

Success of any educational programme depends upon the favourable responses of the teachers and the taught. A favourable and fertile environment is necessary for arousing the positive responsiveness of the members of miniature society of the school and the larger society. So the first and the foremost task in the hands of researchers and planners is to assess the psycho-neural readiness of the individuals of society in general and teachers and students in particular. The Adolescent Education programmes being a new field of education needs the same. From this point of view, the present study is of immense educational value.

The tool used in the present piece of research work will provide a ready-made tool to the research workers and educational planners to measure the value and perceptions of teachers and students. The results of such studies will provide clues for the trends prevailing in the society. So such information can be used for diagnostic and remedial purposes.

Apart from these implications the findings of present study may shed light on the cognitive, emotional and motivational structure of the attitude towards issues related to sex and sexuality.

The SSRVPs tool developed in the present study

may be used by teachers and students for their own evaluation and such evaluation may prove useful, convenient, reliable and valid means for self-improvement for the teachers.

The tool developed can also help in exploring the mental set of teachers and students to accept the educational programme related to adolescence education and sex education.

Findings have suggested that SES has emerged as an important factor in acceptance of sex education. This is important for planning such programme for different classes.

On the issues of gender equality male students show higher agreement than their female counterparts. Female respondents perceive Gender Equality, less agreeable. Curriculum planners could take into consideration this finding while planning sex education/adolescence education or reproductive health curriculum.

Females value virginity more valuable than males at the same time there is trend in favour of premarital sex. In the age of AIDS pandemic where preventive education is the only solution. This part could be dealt in details for its pscychological, moral and reproductive health values.

Students have more stereotyped thinking and it should be addressed in curriculum. In case of myths and misconceptions students are less informed than their teachers. This calls for more informative inservice programmes for the student community. As NPE (1986) emphasised the organisation of preservice and inservice teacher education at district level such programmes are to be need based and socially relevant. These research based INSET programmes shall prove affective for students and teachers.

Curriculum framers of adolescence education can be equipped better if they are provided research based information about the weaker areas of knowledge and attitude for students and teacher training course.

Truth of heterosexual interests has been more boldly acknowledged by students than their teachers. Hence the adult community is yet to accept certain realities related to sex psychology.

The findings of this study can help teachers to understand sexuality and its needs to be dealt with more sympathetically for their students and thus helping reducing generation gap.

Social acceptance of AIDS patients is more in case of teachers than their students. This shows that students need positive attitude building towards of curriculum framers and also of pre-service teacher education and inservice programmes so focus on developing such positive attitude among the students.

For counsellors in schools working with adolescents students findings of their study can be useful in knowing the causes of deviant behaviour having its roots in SSRVPs. They are better equipped professionally if their knowledge is up to date relating to adolescent sexuality, value patters and trends.

Thus, the finding of the study will be useful for researchers, educationists, educational planners and counsellors.

5.4 Suggestions for Further Research

The following suggestions for further research can be given:

1. Researches may be undertaken to identify and to construct valid instrument to measure the SSRVPs of educational administrators, teacher educators, parents who influence SSRVPs of students and teachers.

2. A study of any change over a period of time in SSRVPs of students and teachers can be undertaken.

3. This study can also be used for testing any programme change by conducting pre-test/ post test.

4. Similar study can be conducted to measure the SSRVPs of parents of same students.

5. A detailed study on any of the fifteen variable identified in the present study can be conducted.

6. Study of SSRVPs is extended to other pre-adolescent group of students and post adolescent students.

7. The research could be planned on rural urban differences in students and teaching community of SSRVPs.

8. Similar work could be planned on different cultural and geographical settings.

9. Similar work can also be carried out on the

married and unmarried adolescents.

10. Research could also be conducted to look for any difference in SSRVPs of normal and juvenile/criminal adolescents.

11. Research work could be carried out in detail on the sexual criminology and their SSRVPs patterns.

A number of suggestions can be given but above mentioned seem to be worthy of immediate attention of educational community.

Bibliography

Abbey Harris (1984), Nancy, *Family Life Education: House work for Parents and Teens.* Santa Cruz C.A., Network Publications, p. 79.

Adolescence Education – *Report of the National Seminar.* New Delhi, NCERT, 1994. p. 99.

AIDS and Sexual Behaviour needs of adolescents girls. AIDS in India: New letter of the National AIDS Control Organisation, March 1995: P: 24-27.

Allport, W. (1961) *Patterns & growth in personality.* New York: Holt Rinehart & Winston Inc.

Almedia, D (2001) *'Battle of the Sexes'.* The Times of India, 30th May, 2001 New Delhi

Alosius S. (1974), *A comparative study of the opinion of parents and adolescents towards the introduction of sex education in schools.* Unpublished. M.Ed. Thesis of Bangalore University.

Anand, P. (1963). *Some questions about sex education.* Family Planning. News 4(5): 89.

A summary report of the recommended actions on reproductive health and rights of the ICPD Programme of Action, September 1994, New York, p. 45.

Bahuguna, N.J. (2000). *The Young are left out in Sexual Health Schemes.* Asian Age. 3.9.2000.

Balasubramaniam, K. et.al. (1970). *A study of the reaction of high school teachers to population education as an integral part of the school curriculum.* Journal of Family Welfare. 17(2). 47-51.

Baldwin, J.D.,Whiteley, S., & Baldwin, J.I. (1992). The effect of ethnic group on sexual activities related to contraception and STDs. Journal of Sex Research, 29(2), 189-205.

Bansal, R.K., *Sexual Behaviour and Substance use patterns among adolescents truck cleaners and risk of HIV/AIDS.* Indian Journal of Maternal and Child Health. 1992. Oct-Dec. 3(4): 108-10.

Basnayake, Sriani (1986), *Knowledge and attitude about reproductive health among youth in Sri Lanka;* a study in selected urban and rural communities. Colombo, Family Planning of Sri Lanka. Occasional Publication.

Bhattacharya, M., Joshi, P.L. Teenage Pregnancy: *Present Trends and Future Prospects.* Workshop on Strategy Formulation to Reduce Teenage Fertility in UP, India. Final Report edited by Gupta and Joshi. Nainital, U.P. Academy of Administration. pp. 33-36.

Bhatwadekar & Israel (1970) *Educational Documentation & Information.* UNESCO

Bigner, J.J. (1983). *Human Development: A Life Span Approach.* New York: Macmillon: Publishing Co.

Bishop, P.D., & Lipsitz, A. (1991). Sexual behavior among college students in the AIDs era: A comparative study. Journal of Psychology and Human Sexuality, 3, 35-52.

Brown, A.G. (1974) *Population Education sponsored by the Family Plannig Association of Hongkong as part of World Population Year Programme.* Hongkong.

Brown Lorna Ed. (1981). *Sex Education in the Eighties: the Challenges of Healthy Sexual Evolution,* New York, Plenum Press. p. 264 USA.

Brown, S.V. (1985). Premarital sexual permissiveness among black adolesdent females. Social Psychology Quarterly, 48, 381-387.

Chauliac, M. Raimbault, A.M. (1992) *Adolescence Pregnancy.* (La grossess chez l'adolescente. Development Et.Sante; (98): 235.

Chhabra, S. *A Step Towards Helping Mothers with Unwanted Pregnancies.* Indian Journal of Maternal and Child. 1992, April-June; 3(2): 41-42.

Chhabra, S. (1993). *Adolescent mother .... an unprepared child.* Indian Journal of Maternal and Child Health. 1993. July-September; 4)3): 67-70.

Chugh, S. (1998). Article *'That's Not True'.* The Times of India, 4.4.1998.

C.H. and Winifred M.Whiteley (1967), *Sex and Morals*, London, B.T. Batsford Ltd.

Cobliner, W.G. (1988). The exclusion of intimacy in the sexuality of the contemporary college-age population. Adolescence, 23 (89), 99-113.

Collin, G. (1986), *Becoming the best you can be, A students text book*. Granville, Ohio, Quest International. Skills for Adolescence.

Cormach, M.L. (1961) *She who Rides a Peacock Indian Students and Social Change*. Bombay. Asia Publishing House

Crow & Crow (1965). *Adolescent Development and Adjustment*. 2nd Edition. New York. Mcgraw Hill, 1965. P. IX. 523.

Dahleez (1994), a population education programme on Yuvavani. Focus on Population, environment, Development, 1994, April-June; 8(2):5.

Davis, J.A., & Smith, T.W. (1987). General social surveys, 1972-1988. Chicago: National Opinion Research Center.

DeLamater, J.D., & MacCorquodale, P. (1979). Premarital sexuality: Attitudes, relationships, behaviors. Madison : University of Wisconsin Press.

Education Department, Hongkong (1986). *Guidelines on Sex Education in Secondary Schools*. Hong Kong.

Family Care International (1994). *A summary report of the recommended action on reproductive health and rights of the Cairo, ICPD Programme of Action*, September 1994. New York. p. 45.

Family Planning Association of Hong Kong. Family Life Education: *Handbook for Teachers.* 2nd edition. Hong Kong.

Fathalla, Mohmud F. (1990), Eds. & Others. *Reproductional Health: Global issues.* Park Ridge. N.J. Parthenon Publshing Group. (The Figo Manual of Human Reproduction, V. 3.

Firestein, B.A. (2000), *Bisexuality*: The Psychology and Politics of an Invisible Minority. Inclination Education and Profem.

Gallagher, Mary & Others (1996). *Role of Adolescent Perceptions in Personal and Social Education.* A Review of Literature. Journal of Curriculum Studies, Vol.28, No.5, pp. 577-596.

Gangrade, K.D. (1975). *Population Education for University Youths.* A Research-cum-Action Study. FPFI. New Delhi.

Garrett H.E., Woodworth R.S. (1981), *Statistics in Psychology & Education.* Bombay: Vakils, Feffer & Simons Pvt. Ltd.

Gee (1950), *Social Science Research Methods,* New York: Appleton Century – Crafts Inc., 1950.

George Fr. Dr. (1994) *'Sexual Morality'.* Palack Pillay, SDB, Secretary. All India Don Bosco Education Society

Government of India (1993). *Education for All*: The Indian Scene. Department of Education. MHRD. Government of India. New Delhi.

Gozzer, G. (1990). *School Curricula & social Problems*: Prospects. Vol.XX. No.1. France

Guilford, J.P. (1950), *Fundamental Statistics in*

Psychology and Education, New York: McGraw-Hill Book Compnay Inc.

Gupta R.B.; Khan M.E. – *Teenage Fertility in UP*: Some results from Baseline Survey in Uttar Pradesh. A Report organised by UP Academy of Administration, Nainital 15-16 May (1995) edited by R.B.Gupta, Suresh Joshi. Nainital, India, UP Academy of Administration, 1995; 30-32.

Gupta, R.B. (1974) Variations in the age structure of India population during 1961-1971, Demography India (Delhi) 306-314, December

Gupta, R.B.; Khan, M.E. (1995). Teenage fertility in U.P.: Some results from baseline survey in Uttar Pradesh. A report organised by UP Academy of Administration, Nainital. 15-16 May edited by R.B. Gupta, Suresh Joshi. Nainital, India, UP Academy of Administration, 1995; 30-32.

Gurrusibm K.C. (1965) *Psychology of Adolescence*: London: Prentice Hall Inc.

Hall, G.S. (1904) *Adolescence: Its Psychology and Its Relations to Physiology, Anthropology, Sociology, Sex, Crime, Religion and Education.* New York: Appleton Century Crafts.

Hall, Lynn & Thomas Modl Eds. (1988). *AIDS: Opposing View Points.* St. Paul Minn, Green Haven Press. p. 223.

Harrison, D.E., Bennett, w.H., Globetti, G., & alsikafi, M. (1974)- Premarital sexual standards of rural youth. Journal of Sex Research, 10, 266-277.

Hendrick, C. & Hendrick, S.S. (1988). Lovers wear

rose colored glasses. Journalof Social and Personal Relationships, 5, 161-183.

Hendrick, S.S., & Hendrick, C. (1987a). Love and sex attitudes: A close relationship. In W.H. Jones & D. Perlman (Eds.), Advances in personal relatonships (pp. 141-169). Greenwich, CT: JAI.

Hendrick, S.S., & Hendrick, C. (1987b). Love and sexual attitudes, self- disclosure,and sensation-seeking. Journal of Social and Personal Relationships, 4, 281-297.

Hendrick, S.S. & Hendrick, C. (1987c). Multidimensionality of sexual attitudes. Journal of Sex Research, 23, 502-526.

Inderjeet, Sabina (1995), *No to Sex Education in Schools*. The Times of India. 21 Sept. 1995. New Delhi.

International Planned Parenthood Federation (1985). Programme development department. *Growing up in a changing world*, Part one: youth organisation and family life education: An Introduction. London.

Isadore Rubin and Deryek Calderwood (1973), *Family Guide to Sex*, New York, The New America Library, Inc.

Israel, S. *Problems of Sex Education* (1964). Journal of Association of Medical Women in India (Delhi) 52: 90-92, Nov.1964.

Jain K. (1995), *Survey shows Delhi School Children Sexually Active*; The Times of India. Article. 27.02.1995.

John t.Zadrozmy (1959), *Dictionary of Social Science*,

Washington D.C., Public Affairs Press.

Julius Gould and William L.Kolb (1964), *A Dictionary of the Social Sciences*, New York, The Free Press

Kakodkar P.'*Talking Sex to Children*'. The Times of India. October 28, 1995.

Kala, Arvind, The Hindustan Times, September 6, 1995, '*Worm in the Apple*'. Article.

Kalra R.M. & Kalra S. (1999) *Adolescents & AIDS a new Generation at Risk*. p.141. Vikas Publishing House.

Kasun Jacqueline R. Condom Nation: *Government Sex Education promotes teen pregnancy*. Policy review No. 68. Spring 1994. 79-82. Washington D.C.

Kaul, M. (2000) *Arrangement Marriages Bounce Back*. The Times of India. September 3, 2000. New Delhi

Khan, R.S. (2000), (Ed.) *Population Education – Content and Methodology*. IASE, Jamia Millia Islamia.

Kazmi, N. (2000), *When Will Men Grow Up*? The Times of India. 18.2.2000. New Delhi.

King, K., Balswick, J.O., & Robinson, I.E. (1977). The continuing premarital sexual revolution among college females. Journal of Marriage and the Family, 39, 455-459.

Kilpatrick, C. (1980). Sex roles and sexual satisfaction in women. Psychology of Women Quarterly, 4, 444-459.

Lawton, D. (Ed.) 1971). *Population Education and the Younger Generation*. London. International Planned Parenthood Federation. p. 85.

Llewellyn, J. & Derek (1998). *Understanding Sexuality*, Melbourne, Oxford University Press. p. 136. Australia

Madaras, L. (1986). Lynda Madaras' *growing up guide for girls*. New York. New Market Press. USA

Maheshwari, S.B. (1972). *A study of the reaction of teacher towards the introduction of population education in schools*. (M.Ed. Dissertation). Jamia Millia Islamia. New Delhi. 120 p. (unpublished)

Maitra, N. (1994). Sex Roles. Bib.Sr.8. *Adolescence Education*. p. 82-84. NCERT.

Manorama H.S. (1990) India: *Sex Education Counselling Research Training*. Bibliography Sr.8. Adolescence Education, NCERT, pp.46-48.

Manorama, H.S. (1990). India: *Sex Education Counselling Research Training Therapy*/Family Life and Marriage Counselling Centre. Planned Parenthood in Europe. December.

Margolin, L (1989). Gender and the preorgatives of dating and marriage. An experimental assessment of a sample of college students. Sex Roles, 20, 91-102.

Matanagnon, R. (1982). Sex and the Filipino Adolescent: A Review, Phillipine Studies. 30: 311-334. UNESCO.

Muehlenhard, C.L. (1988). "Nice women" don't say yes and " real men" don't say no: How miscommunication and the double standard can cause sexual problems. Women and Therapy, 7, 95-108.

Muehlenhard, C.L., & Quackenbush, D.M. (1988, November). Can the sexual double standard put women at risk for sexually transmitted diseases? The role of the double standard in condom use among women. Paper presented at the Annual Meeting of the society for the Scientific Study of Sex, San Francisco, CA.

Mc Cary, J. (1973). *Human Sexuality Physiological, Psychological and Sociological Factors.* 2nd Ed. Van Norstad, New York. USA. p. 542.

Mehta, Saxena & Mukherjee (1969) Educational documentation & information. UNESCO Paris (Geneva)

Mehta (1974). *Population growth and population oriented education in population education for teacher.* NCERT. pp. 43-52.

Mehta, G.L. (1974). *A study of the opinion of parents and teachers towards introduction of population education in high schools of Bhubaneswar.* M.Ed. Dissertation (unpublished). Utkal University.

MHRD, National Policy on Education. 1986. New Delhi: MHRD (Ministry of Education), Government of India. 1986.

MHRD, *Programme of Action* (NPE-I, 1986), MHRD (Ministry of Education), Government of India. 1986.

Mohan & Shree Venkatram (1997) *The AIDS Epidemic: Research and Testing Need Urgent Attention.* The Times of India. March 19. New Delhi.

Mukhi, Sarla (1987). *Problems in Adolescents Sexuality.* Bombay. Family Plannig Association of India (1987). [p. 17.

Muley D.S. (1999), *Population and Adolescence*

Education – A Training Package. Population and Development Cell. CBSE. New Dellhi.

Myrdal, Alva. (1968). Nation and family. *The Swedish experiment in democratic family and population policy.* Cambridge Massachusetts Institute of Technology Press. p. 441.

Nagpal, J. (2001), *The Capital Story, Hindustan Times,* 13th May, 2001, New Delhi.

Nag, Moni (1972). *Sex culture and human fertility.* Current Anthropology 13(2): 231-37. April.

Nag, Moni (1994). *Sexual Behaviour and AIDS in India:* State of the Art. Indian Journal of Social Work IV (4). October, 1994: 43.

Nagda, S. (1972). *Population education measuring and definition in population education seminar.* Bhopal: FPAI (1972).

Nagda, L. et.al (1975). A survey of the perception of the students of the womens' college towards Population Education News Letter. Population Study Centre. S.V.University.

National Crime Records Bureau Report (1992), Government of India.

*National Seminar (*1995)*-cum-Workshop on Value Education* (1995) New Delhi; CBSE & Bharatiya Vidya Bhawan.

NCERT (1974). *Population Education – Selected Readings.* New Delhi. 1974.

NCERT, *Fourth All India Educational Survey,* New Delhi: NCERT.

NCERT, *Fifth All India Educational Survey,* Volume I. New Delhi: NCERT

NCERT. *National Bibliography on Population Education.*

New Delhi. 1975.

NCERT. *Adolescence Education.* Abs. Bibliography. Population Doc. Services: Bibliography, Sr. No. 8.

NCERT. *Adolescence Education in Schools.* Adolescence Education: Knowledge Base. New Delhi. 1999.

NCERT (1981). *A Decade of Population Education Research in India:* A Status Study. New Delhi.

NCERT (1993). *Population Education Research in India: Inventory and Analysis.* NCERT, New Delhi.

NCTE (1998). *Population and Reproductive Health Education;* A Training Package. NCTE. New Delhi.

Oommen, T.K. *Family in Transition. Patterns of Response to change.* The Times of India. December 17, 1990.

Oser, F.K. & Patry, J.L. opine that *students can be taught to become responsible by the teachers.*

Pandey J.L. (1999), *Adolescence Education.* Indian Journal of Population Education. April-September, 1999. New Delhi.

Patel, P. (1974). *A study of knowledge and attitude towards human reproduction among eleventh grade students in some urban schools.* Thesis. M.S.University Baroda. Faculty of Education and Psychology. p. 90.

Patel, V. (1971). *A study of population awareness of standard X at Varnama High School.* Thesis (MS). M.S. University of Baroda. Faculty of Education and Psychology. p. 103.

Peplau, L.A., Rubin, Z., & Hill, C.T. (1977). Sexual

intimacy in dating relationships, Journal of Social Issues, 33, 86-109.

Population Education Research in India (1981-1990). Inventory and Analysis, NPEU, New Delhi – NCERT.

Prahallada B. (1971). A study of knowledge and attitude towards human reproduction among.

Prahallada, N.N. (1994), *Contemporary Significance of Value Education,* University News, February 14, 1999.

Pratinidhi, Natu & Joshi (1991). *Perimarital Counselling on Family Planning, Health & Population – Perspective and Issues.* Jul-Dec.; 14(3-4); 118-24.

Ramachandra (1974). *A study of the knowledge and attitude of teachers of Kurnool towards Population Education.* Newsletter of the Population study centre. Sri Venkateshwara University.

Rao D.Gopal (1972). *Needed Research in Population Education in Mehta & Chandra (Eds.). Population Education – Selected readings.* New Delhi. NCERT. pp.136-139.

Rao, D.G. (1976). *A study of the attitudes of parents and teachers towards sex education.* Population Education Unit, NCERT, New Delhi.

Rao (1974). *Population growth & socio-economic developments – the Indian case. Demography India. 3(2): 209-221.*

Raymundo, C.M. (1984) *Young Adult Fertility in the Philippines: First report. Manila, Population Institute, University of the Philippines.* 76 P.

Abs.Bib.Sr.7. Bangkok. UNESCO.

Reiss, I.L. (1960). Premarital sexual standards in America. New York : Free Press.

Reiss, I.L. (1964). The scaling of premarital sexual permissiveness. Journal of Marriage and the Family, 26, 188-198.

Report on the family life education survey: Family Planning Association of Hong Kong. A study of Hong Kong School Youth.

Robert M.Goldenson (1984), *Longman Dictionary of Psychology and Psychiatry*, New York, Longman

Rogers, Dorothy (1977). *Psychology of Adolescence*. Englwood Cliff. New Jersey, Prentice Hall. 1977. P.552.

Rome Harre and Roger Lamb (1986), Ed; *The Dictionary of Personality and Social Psychology*, Oxford, Baṇi Blackwell Ltd.

Ruhela, S.P. (1969) *Sociology of Sex Education in India*, Delhi Dhanpat Rai & Sons

Ryan & Cooper. *Those Who Can Teach*. 1996. 7th Edition. New York

Sadiq N. (2000), *A Few Thoughts for the New Century*. UNFPA. Executive Director on International Women's Day, March 8, 2000

Sami Ahmad, S. (1994), *The Importance of Sex Education*. The Times of India. October 20, 1994.

Sangwan, S. (2001). *Growing up in a Bigger, Badder World*, Hindustan Times, 13th May, 2001, New Delhi

Sebald, Hans. (1984) *Adolescence: a social*

psychological analysis. 3rd Ed. New Jersey. Prentice Hall, Inc. P.336.

SECRT. *Attitudes and Perceptions of Educated Urban Youth to Marriage and Sex.* FPAI. Bombay

Seshadri, C. et.al. (1992) *Education in Values.* A Source Book. New Delhi. NCERT

Sharma N. (2000). *Let's Talk About Sex, Not Bees and Birds.* The Asian Age. 10.09.2000. New Delhi

Shapurian, R., & Hojat, M. (1985). Sexual and premarital attitudes of Iranian college students. Psychological Reports, 57, 67-74.

Sherwin, R., & Corbett, S.(1985). Campus sexual norms and dating relationships: A trend analysis. Journal of Sex Research, 21, 258-274.

Singh, B.K. (1980). Trends in attitudes toward premarital sexual relations. Journal of Marriage and the Family, 42, 387-393.

Shukla, R.P. (1997), *Towards Developing Values Among Children. An Analytical Approach,* Journal University News, Vol. 35 No.39, September, 1997.

Snyder, M., Simpson, J.A., & Gangestad, S. (1986). Personality and sexual relations, Journal of Personality and Social Psychology, 51, 181“-190.

Sri Lanka, Department of Census and Statistics. *Socio-economic development and fertility decline in Sri Lanka.* Colombo. 161 P.

Staff Report on Proposal on Sex Education. The Times of India. December 2, 1995.

The Tribune (2000). *Combat AIDS with awareness*, 21st May, 2000, Chandigarh

The Tribune (2000). *H.V – The Positive Approach.* 22.5.2000. Chandigarh

Testa, R.J., Kinder, B.N., & Ironson, G. (1987). Heterosexual bias in the perception of loving relationships of gay males and lesbians. Journal of Sex Research, 23, 163-172.

Thompson, A.P. (1983). Extramarital sex: A review of trhe research literature. Journal of Sex Research, 19, 1-22127. Times of India (1999) *Awareness Can Curb Child Sexual Abuse.* May 2, 1999. New Delhi

UNESCO (1991) *Adolescence Education, Physical Aspect* – Module One – UNESCO: Bangkok

UNESCO (1991) *Adolescence Education, Social Aspect* – Module Two – UNESCO: Bangkok

UNESCO (1991) *Adolescence Education, Physical Aspect* – Module Three – UNESCO: Bangkok

UNESCO (1991) Adolescence Education, Sexually Transmitted Diseases – Module Four – UNESCO: Bangkok

UNESCO (1988) *Family Life & Sex Education.* Abstract Bibliography Sr.9, Bangkok

UNESCO (1986) *Selected Entries on Demography & Its Bearing on Population Education in Seven Asian Countries.* Abstract Bibliography, Sr.7, Bangkok (1986)

UNESCO (1974) *Educational Documentation and Information, Population Education* – Problems and Perspectives. No.193. 4th Quarter 1974. France

UNESCO (1983) *Population Education Programme in Asia:* What Research Says. Abstract Bibliography, Sr.No.4. Bangkok – 1983

UNESCO (1985) *Teaching Methodologies for Population Education,* Regional Office, Bangkok, 1985.

UNESCO (1974). Educational documentation and information Bulletin of the International Bureau of Education. 4th Quarter. No.193. UNESCO. Paris. Geneva.

UNFPA (2000) *Adolescents in India:* A Profile. New Delhi

UNFPA (2000) *Government Announces National Population Policy.* Pop Times. Vol.2 No.1, April, 2000. New Delhi

UNFPA (2000). A few thoughts for the new century. Dr.Nafis Sadiq. UNFPA. Executive Director, on International Women's Day, March 8, 2000.

Unnithan T.K.N. (1998) *Education in Human Values,* University News. December 5, 1988.

Upmanyu, V.V. & Upmanyu Sushma (1994). *Depression in relation to sex role identity and hopelessness among male and female Indian adolescents.* Journal of Social Psychology. Vol. 134. No.4. August 1994. 551-552.

Varghese (1970). Journal of Family Welfare. Vol.16. No.2. December (1970)

Varghese, *P.V. A study of the attitude of teachers towards different aspects of population problems.* M.Ed. Thesis. Bangalore University (Unpublished)

Varma, B.P. *Interaction with environment.* Bib. Sr.8. Adolescence Education. P.49. NCERT.

Varma, B.P (1999). *Dimensions of home environment and adolescents alienation.* Progress of Education. Vol.IXV, No.2. PP.30-33.

Villages M.B. (1996) *The Books of Values.* ING Baring & ING Bank. Philippines. 1996

Wieland, Sandra (1997). *Hearing the Internal Trauma: Working with Children and Adolescents who have been sexually abused.* New Delhi. Pub..P.XV, 232

Walia, A.K. (2000). Delhi Health and Family Welfare Minister in 'National Herald'

Walia, Nona (1999, 21st August), Times of India, in column *'Relationship: Hippie Parents are Embarrassing.* New Delhi

Wieland, Sandra (1997). Hearing the Internal Trauma: Working with Children and Adolescents who have been sexually abused. New Delhi. Pub..P.XV, 232

Weis (2000) *Learning to Speak Out in an Abstinence Based Sex Education Group*: Gender and Race Work in an Urban Magnet School. Teacher College Record Vol.102 No.2, June 2000. PP 620-650. Columbia University

WHO/UNESCO (1989): *A Teaching Guide for Secondary Schools:* Suva, Fiji (Office of the Regional Advisor for Population Education in the Pacific) Fiji.

Winer, B.J. (1962) *Statistical Principles in Experimental Design*, McGraw Hill Book Compnay Inc. New York

World Health Organisation (1993), *Health of young people: A challenge and a promise.* Geneva. p. 109.

Yarber, L. (1978) AIDS: *What Young Adults Should Know;* Students Guide. Virginia, U.S.A.

Yadav, R.C. (1995). *Sexual Behaviour.* Bib.Sr.8. Adolescence Education. P.52-61. NCERT.

Index

F

G

H

I

J

K

L

M